Ask the Silence

WHEN YOU NEED TO BELIEVE
SOMETHING EXTRAORDINARY
MUST HAPPEN

~~Love Story~~

WHEN YOU NEED TO BELIEVE
SOMETHING EXTRAORDINARY
MUST HAPPEN

Printed in the United States of America

First Printing, 2017

ISBN 978-0-9988830-1-4

Love Story, LLC
950 Third Avenue – 11th Floor
New York, New York 10022

www.LoveStoryWriter.com

CONTENTS

INTRODUCTION

I DIDN'T EVEN KNOW THERE WAS A BOTTLE UNTIL THE GENIE POPPED OUT

WHAT HAPPENS WHEN you come to the end of all of your resources and have nothing left, *but somehow you find a way to keep going?*

I've been in this same place, but different situations, many times in my life, and it's not always fun, but these situations deliver some of the most valuable gifts I've ever been given, and it wasn't until it was explained to me here, in a book that *I* wrote, that I started to understand what was happening.

What you are reading never was intended to be a book; it was meant to help me feel better about something I did and am completely responsible for. I am committed to making this a blessing to everyone, and not only to those who are involved, but hopefully to everyone reading these words, as well. Making this a blessing to those who are directly affected would require a commitment far beyond that of any legal obligation, and this is exactly what I am doing every day of my life, and I won't stop until I feel satisfied that I have successfully completed what I have been trusted to complete—successful by *my* standards, which would be more than anyone could possibly expect of me. I'm tempted to say what I felt before this book wrote me, that I made a huge, devastating mistake that caused me to experience more pain than I ever had before.

However, after reading through the conversation that follows, I came back to revise this introduction because I no longer feel the same way after the explanation I received from a part of me that I never knew existed. Initially, it was the most difficult thing I had ever had to deal with because the one thing I wanted to get right in my life was to not hurt the ones I love the most. My initial devastation and the greatest pain I have ever experienced have been replaced by a level of commitment to give everything I have, every day, to accomplish something I cannot live without accomplishing. At the time I am writing this, only two people know what I'm talking about. The two people who work with me every day know something about what I do daily and how much this means to me. They have access to sites that contains my long-term as well as hourly goals every day. I could not be more blessed to have in my corner, a team so intelligent, resourceful, and committed to my mission as I fight daily to make this happen.

I started writing on May 4, 2010. On that day, I created a community page on Facebook to anonymously express how I felt about someone I loved but couldn't be with. In time, my readers started calling me "Love Story." My pages became an outlet through which I could express what I have learned from my life journey, as well as who I have become in the process.

At the end of the summer of 2014, I was sitting in my apartment reflecting on my entire life, especially the previous two years I had lived in New York City. I have had many extreme changes in my life. I knew another one was coming, but I wasn't yet quite sure what it would be. I told my best friend that I wanted to live in a cabin in the woods away from all people so I could write and connect to this *thing* I connect to when I'm alone. I was not sure what it was at the time, but I've had some amazing experiences with it at different stages of my life. I always thought it was interesting that whenever I knew I wanted to write something, it was usually never an idea, but a *feeling*, and I was not sure what would come of it. It was initially difficult to direct the feeling to a subject I wanted to write about, but eventually this ability began to develop. Even when I had some idea of what to write about, the feeling would usually take over and write about something else. So, in the very beginning, I had almost no control of the words that came out.

From many experiences I had while I was growing up, I knew there was much more to us than anyone was aware of, and I seemed to intuitively know that a large part of my life would be spent exploring this amazing power. I was fascinated by what I and others were able to do when connected to it, and the feeling is something I cannot accurately describe using words, although I do the best I can to describe it in this book. A variety of factors came together almost simultaneously that prompted my decision to leave New York City and find a quiet place to write and connect to what I now call my soul. Ultimately, I realized that what I connect to is much more than my soul.

With the help of a friend, I started to realize that my life had not been real and that, contrary to popular opinion, this was not a bad thing; it was the blessing I needed so that I could realize that I was on an adventure to authenticity. I wanted my life to be real, but it is not as easy as people think. Being honest with yourself is much, much harder than anyone can imagine. To be honest about who you are and *why* you do what you do is the key to an authentic life. Getting there is a long road, but I know that eventually we all choose authenticity, and this was my time.

It took me a long time to even want to move in this direction. I have made what I believe to be huge progress, and yet I know I still have mountains to climb in this new world. Knowing how far I have to go is not at all discouraging, but on the contrary, very exciting. I look forward to the time when my life will unfold without putting me through so much pain.

Please don't get me wrong here: I *love* my life. I would not change one thing that I have done or that has already happened, because I realize that by doing so, I am saying that I don't like who I am today or that I want to be someone else, and that is just not true. I wish there were a way to become who I am without hurting so many people. Who I am is far from perfect, but I love who I am and where I'm going. I know this is not easy to understand and will be especially so once you know the situation I am in as I write this.

There was a time I would have wanted my problem to magically vanish or wished that I could rewind and do everything differently. Now, although I do not ever want to repeat my "failures," "mistakes," or whatever else they might be called, I love where I am right now. Even knowing the possible consequences of my current situation, *I still do not want to change what already has happened.* This doesn't mean I want to do it again, it just means that I now understand how it blesses me, everyone involved, and possibly the entire world depending on what I do from here. And also, depending on how others react, or better yet, *respond* to the language of feeling in their situations and to their pain.

I know you don't understand this now, but I promise you, if you make a study of this book instead of just reading it and tossing it aside, you *will* understand why I feel this way. Also, in your understanding of it, you will discover your true purpose in life. You will discover the real meaning of your life and the reason you are here—and I'm not referring to what you do for a living or even your greatest passion. We will talk about your *path* to your purpose and how it always runs through your heart.

When I was a young kid, I was afraid of everything and everyone. I was so afraid to speak that I developed a serious stuttering problem. I avoided people and conversations whenever

I could. School was torture for me for many reasons, and you will learn one of those reasons in this book.

Every mother in the world knows how painful it is to give birth to their most beautiful gift. I have come to learn that a gift of mine was being born out of tremendous pain, but who could possibly have had the vision to see this while it was happening? Certainly not me, and not anyone I was aware of. What good could possibly come from being terrified of everyone and everything? The answer: A love for being alone. I now look at being socially awkward when I was younger as a gift that guaranteed I would find silence. My desire to avoid conversations, and people in general, led me to spend a lot of time by myself.

In the beginning, I just didn't want to talk to anyone; eventually, though, I came to crave alone time, as if it were air. Some secret attraction to being alone never left me, and it took me half a century to figure it out. Stillness has its own intelligence, its own peace, and its own love. I have been led to silence through every painful event in my life, and this is what makes these painful events my greatest blessings. The pain has continued, and yet I *know* that something beautiful is being born from it. Something beautiful already has been born from the situation I'm in, and I know there is much more to come. There is no question. There is no doubt. I don't have to ask anyone or look anything up, although I do have spiritual mentors who are not consciously aware that they mentor me and one who surely does. Seclusion and silence summon my greatest mentor.

My journey has been a truly rewarding journey, but it has not been easy. I could have chosen a much simpler and easier path, but there was so much inside me that I had to get out. My journey always has been a journey to authenticity, although it took me a long time to be aware of that, but once I was consciously aware, it was easier to see how every event and person that comes into my life serves that purpose, and even more so when I don't like it. I have done everything to great extremes, which has taken me down the path to realization and enlightenment much more quickly, but this has come at a truly hefty price. Although I have come a very long way, I have much further to go. Enlightenment is not a destination; I will never get there, but I will always be on my way.

What you are reading is my gift, not because it has value to anyone else, although I hope it does, but because it is my greatest love.

I was born in the Bronx, New York. I grew up in Yonkers and lived in New York City for two years and nine months. I seemed to need more time alone than ever, so I moved from the twenty-fourth floor of a Manhattan apartment to a place that looks and feels like my own planet. For most of the time I wrote this book, I lived in a Hogan in Navajo country, near what is called the Four Corners (the intersection of Arizona, New Mexico, Colorado, and Utah).

A Hogan is a small octagon, the front door of which always faces the sunrise. Where I lived, there were no streets or addresses for many miles. The floor of my home was red sand, and there was no running water anywhere in the area. It was a fifty-two-mile round trip to town, where I bought cases of bottled water so I could take a "shower" by pouring them over my head. I lived in a place where I had to figure out the necessities of life, and it was very good for me. I even had to chop wood just to stay warm. The people who had known me just one year earlier would not believe I would ever do this.

Where I lived, there were no trees, so I wasn't chopping down trees, but at times a piece of firewood would be too big to fit in my wood-burning stove, so I had to cut it. I could drive for miles and not see one person, one car, or any signs of human life. I lived among horses, donkeys, cattle, rabbits, and some magical birds. I had neighbors on each side of me (the owners of the property), but there were times I didn't see any of them for many months. Living in a place like this made it easier for me to connect to my soul, and it was the change I needed in my life.

Although when my soul speaks, I'm connected to a world I don't recognize as me, this book is not channeled —and you will find out why when you read it. This was a huge revelation to me, because I had been saying for a long time that everyone with a heartbeat is a channeler. We don't just *have* our own soul; we *are* our own soul. And we don't just have access to the soul of God or the soul of the universe, we are the soul of God and we are the soul of the universe.

What you call *you*, your soul, and the soul of God are not three different entities; they are three different parts of the same entity.

Before my most devastating failure, I had gotten to a place where I really believed I would never be concerned with worry again. I really thought I had conquered worry for good, but when "this" happened, it was killing me. I had never messed up to a degree even close to this in my entire life, and that would seem something of an endorsement if you looked closely enough at my hundreds of epic screw-ups.

After what happened, I was having trouble sleeping. Somehow, I never seemed to think about what my punishment might be, but maybe that's because I was living the punishment. The only thing that mattered to me was fixing the problem as fast as I could.

Home at my place where there were no people around for miles, one night I was looking up at the stars and was filled with the most peaceful feeling I had ever experienced. I felt that God had given me this gift of peace. The contrast to what I had been feeling just an instant before made it even more spectacular. I felt I was being spoken to by the stars, as if they were alive and telling me that everything was okay, that it was supposed to be this way, and that I'm not a failure, not a bad person. I really didn't understand completely. Just as when my soul speaks to me, there were no words, no voice. It was as if the stars had a syringe filled with liquid thought that was powered by emotion; the injection was invisible, but crystal-clear.

I felt great for one night, but when I awoke the next morning, I was still afraid. I was afraid I had done something that I couldn't undo, something that I wasn't able to fix. In an attempt to feel better and regain some hope, I watched some YouTube videos of Abraham Hicks and Neale Donald Walsch. The Neale Donald Walsch video I watched mentioned Byron Katie. Although I had watched the video before and had never looked up Byron Katie, now I really needed answers, so I didn't have the luxury of overlooking anything. When I looked her up and found out about "The Work," I knew it was exactly what I needed.

"The Work" is a process of inquiry that she created to help people feel better about anything. "The Work" is a way to get to the real truth, and that was what was so enticing to me that I decided to try it, but when I did, something even more miraculous happened. I started with one question and never got to any of the others, because what I thought I was imagining turned into a real conversation in which "Byron Katie" told me things I had never heard before. It was completely unexpected. I didn't really understand what was happening. I was not channeling someone from beyond, because Byron Katie is still alive. So, what was I doing and how was I doing it? These questions and so many more will be answered in this book.

Here is the conversation with "Byron Katie." I still don't completely understand what happened, except that something came alive, and it wasn't anything or anyone I recognized at the time.

(BK) You cannot fix this situation in the next twelve months from where you are now—is this true?

(LS) I would not say that it's true, because I know I can, I'm just not sure how to do this from where I stand now.

(BK) You write about this and communicate it so eloquently and with such certainty. What would you say to your daughter or best friend? How would you advise them if they were in your exact position right now? This situation you are in is such a great opportunity for you to, in your own words, "realize who you've always been." Do you see that? Do you also see how what you call your suffering can change the paradigm of the entire world?

(LS) Wow! It is amazing that you said this. I have been thinking in this direction, but you put it in a way I have not thought of before. Thank you so much!

(BK) Anytime. But you are thanking me for "your" words, dear. This is your opportunity to communicate by example what you communicate so perfectly in words, while at the same time giving yourself the gift of realization. Do you see how this "horrible" situation is really the greatest present you've ever been given?

(LS) I do! I really do see it, but I have some work to do before I get to open it.

(BK) The hardest part has already been done, and if you ever have any questions about what to do next, just read your own work. I believe your own work says that you get to open this present right now. Am I wrong in this?

(LS) No, you are so right! At times, I forget who we all are and have to be reminded when it comes to me. Communicating something and acting it out are clearly on different levels.

(BK) You believe what you write, don't you? I love what you write, and I certainly believe in it!

(LS) I really do believe in it fully, and thank you, I love that you believe in it, too.

(BK) Do what you believe in, dear. I know you've done this before.

(LS) Yes, but certainly not on this level.

(BK) Is there a level your philosophy does not work with?

(LS) Touché.

(BK) You have persuaded so many people to believe things that they were never able to believe before; now, it's time for you to get yourself to believe at a level even you are not accustomed to. You are ready for this, dear, or you would not be here.

(LS) Are you starting to rhyme things, now, like I do?

(BK) Of course not. Did you forget you are both of us here?

(LS) Thank you for this. I really needed it. It was incredible. I kind of feel like my entire identity is riding on what I do now.

(BK) I have not done anything here. My words and yours are all yours.

(LS) Thank you very much for whatever part you played, even if it was only your imagined identity in this interaction. Okay, wish me luck!

(BK) You don't need any. You are ready for this, and I believe in you. Now, you just need to get you to believe in you. I can't wait to hear about the success of this story.

(LS) I promise you will!

Now, Byron Katie doesn't know me or anything about this conversation, at least not consciously. I thought to myself, "If this can really happen, what is it about us that makes something like this possible?" Well, you are about to find out.

Imagine that you have failed more than any person who has ever walked this planet. Your one super-achievement was projecting an image of success that everyone believed, and now you find yourself in a place where your greatest failure has put you in the most horrible and embarrassing position you have ever been in, and the only way out is to actually become who you have so successfully pretended to be for more than half a century.

This is my life right now, and this is the absolute truth as I see it, but there is much more to it, as you will surely see. I had myself fooled and had no idea what I was doing.

I now think I understand why Neale Donald Walsch's first book, *Conversations with God,* has been my all-time favorite. *Conversations with God,* books one and three, have always been hard for me to put down. I know that something within me has been wanting to emerge for a long time, and I know now that neither Walsch nor I are the "chosen" ones; we all are the chosen ones, including all of you. There is nothing I have that you don't. We may be unique in certain ways, but you will learn in this book that not only can you connect to this part of you, but you do—all the time, only in ways you consider "nothing special," because everyone else does, too.

You will hear how I connected as a kid in different ways, and you will see how you can connect to this part of you in anything you choose. You will also recognize how you already connect but do not yet see.

In this book, you will learn about love from the master of the universe, and I do *not* mean me—or do I? I mean that part of me and *all* of you that we don't recognize as *us,* yet.

I have mentioned some of what I hope my readers will get out of this book, but it is my deepest desire that the pain from my life will, at the very least, help take the pain away from yours. And, if you have the courage and enough faith to listen to what your heart and soul are saying and respond to them in action, you might even change the world. If not, you will surely change *your* world, which, by the way, is the same thing.

DIALOGUE WITH MY SOUL

HOW WILL I EVER SOLVE THIS PROBLEM?

*I promise, you are more alone in a room full of people
than you are when you "think" you can't find a soul.*

—*Your Soul*

(LS) MY DEAR Soul, you know all you need to know about
me, so please tell me where I go from here? How do I deal with
all I need to do in my situation?

(My Soul) I do know where you go from here, and by the
way, so do you. Based on what you write, is this the appropriate
question to ask me?

(LS) What do you mean?

(My Soul) You know exactly what I mean.

(LS) I do, but then you wouldn't be helping me, and I would
be back on my own again.

(My Soul) You know it's not possible for me to misunderstand
you. You've been saying that you want to take care of this on
your own. I don't just listen to what your words are saying. I feel
your desires with you, so there is no chance I can be even the
slightest bit wrong.

(LS) I do want to take care of this on my own, but I just

thought maybe you could give me some advice. At times, it can be scary to be completely alone.

(My Soul) Do you really not know what to do next? Are you pretending you do when speaking to your fans? You speak with such confidence, such *knowing*—where is that now? Do you truly believe in all you say and write? Are you really completely alone?

(LS) I do know what to do, and no, I'm not pretending, but when I'm in a really scary situation, something that's really hard for me, specifically, to deal with, I have a hard time. I'm having a hard time with this, although I'm handling it much better than I ever would have at any other time in my past. I know I'm not completely alone, but at times it feels that way.

(My Soul) What you call your "biggest screw-up ever" is your greatest gift, but let's be honest here: what is bothering you is the way you will be *seen* because of it. You keep telling people that you're over being seen in a specific way, but you're not, and what you call your "predicament" is meant to reveal this to you, among many other revelations. Do you see this? Is this starting to make sense to you?

(LS) Oh, my God, I never thought of it that way.

(My Soul) The energy and level of commitment that has come from what you see as your greatest disaster enhances your journey on every level. It is intended to make you more in many areas of your life. I have heard you say that this is meant to make all of your dreams come true, and you're right. Your dreams line up perfectly with my mission for you. Doesn't it feel great to be on purpose?

(LS) It does, it really does, but if I am doing so great, then why am I going through this right now? I've come so far, and I know I have, so why torture me again?

(My Soul) Is this what you call torture? I know you want to be the highest *you* possible, so why even question this?

(LS) I guess the part I am still having a problem with is…if

I've become what I've meant to because of all I've done and the way I've lived life, why make me pay for who I no longer am?

(My Soul) You are *not* who you were meant to become. I'm not trying to hurt you, here. You have certainly come a very long way. This is God's way of carving the masterpiece of *you*.

(LS) Well, every time He chisels a piece off, it hurts like hell!

(My Soul) I know you use your GPS almost everywhere you go, but I never thought you'd need one for this conversation. No, you are confusing north with south in a very off-purpose kind of way. "It blesses like heaven" would be more appropriate. I know you have become good at knowing where the messages are coming from and what they're saying, and you even act on them, but you don't always believe your actions. Your message is unparalleled, and it is your choice whether to bring this message to the world. You will be blessing the world and benefiting from it in all ways.

You do listen to your own messages, but when something happens, you disconnect too quickly. You need to work on your own *knowing* some more. You're doing great, you're exactly where you're supposed to be right now. The events of your life have gotten you to be more consistent with writing and working on your dream. I know writing and communicating your unique philosophy to the world is your passion, and you have been given a gift to help you get there. There are not many who would realize this, but I know you do. Most people would not see your current situation as a gift. In fact, many would have taken their lives over what we see as your gift.

You have surely earned the distinction of your new vision, but you're not done yet. You talk about torture as if you're okay with stopping progress here, and we both, or we *one*, however you choose to see us, know that you want to be much more, that you want to *realize* so much more. Everything that has ever happened to you and everything that ever will is, by far, the best possible thing that can happen to you in that moment, at least in terms of growth, or realization. I see you from a much different perspective than you do, and I want you to know that I've felt your pain. You see, I am the part of you that knows everything already is perfect, and I know that nothing has ever happened *to* you, because I am part of the plan that has done all of this *for* you. People have taken what you call their lives right after I have given them their most valuable gifts, and I know exactly where you are right now in your journey to understanding this. Maybe you just need a new pair of glasses.

(LS) I think I will copy that and keep it with me always. Do you really think my message is worth something to the world? Can you tell me if this will be successful?

(My Soul) Why are you pretending to be someone else when you talk to me? You know the answer to the first question, and the second is one only you can choose. If you *choose* that it be successful, it can be nothing else.

(LS) I know it may sound as if I don't believe what I write, but I've never been faced with such a difficult challenge in my entire life. I believe in myself and in my message with all my heart—and *you*—but I live in this time-space reality, and I don't know how much time I have to take care of the matter. I understand why it happened, and I know I have gotten rid of the part of me that caused this, but I've never been under so much pressure to succeed in my life. It's extremely difficult for me to handle, because I never know how much time I have. I could have years or minutes. How do I circumvent time and space to fix all of this—now?

(My Soul) You will, as you say, "fix this" the moment you realize that there is nothing to fix. Your situation could not be more perfect. Nothing is broken, so there is nothing to fix. You are only worried about how everyone will see you and what they will think of you. How can you not know? You have handed them the key to your life, and then you complain about what they say and do when it was *you* who gave their actions and words not only validation, but permission to hurt you. The key you have handed them is not a physical one, so you can take it back anytime you choose, but taking it back would mean that you finally *know* who you are.

I know you have your moments of strength, but it's time for you to be in a committed relationship with peace. I promise that when you say, "I do," this time, you won't be disappointed. Only things that are not related to peace can disappoint. What I mean is, you go to bed with peace, you wake up with peace, you are with peace all day, every day, and she never leaves you.

Can you *realize* who you are in the face of everyone's displeasure about you? Can you display it with *knowing*? This challenge is your greatest gift, and it will reveal yourself to you. In many ways, every moment now, it already is revealing itself. How much do you believe in yourself? How much do you believe who you really are? Do you see how your *realization* is dependent upon your belief, upon your *knowing*? You cannot realize who you already are until you know that you are. In reality, you are everything that you and I have ever dreamed of, but you can only see yourself as far as your belief will take you. Therefore, the reality of you is one thing and your perception of you is another.

All of this can be changed in an instant, and all you have to do is choose a higher belief. Your choosing a higher belief, or more appropriately, a higher *knowing*, will make your dreams come true, as well as my dreams for you. By the way, my dreams for you are not dreams in the sense that you think of them. My dreams for you are never hopes, and they are not even desires in terms of possibilities; they are *realities* from the moment your heart conceived them.

This is also true of your heart. Your heart has desires only in terms of choices, never in terms of what might be possible or not. *We* (your heart and I) never think in terms of something being possible, because we know it is already real. I have told you this many times before, and you have even written about it in different words, but it is all the same truth. There can be no better system. Everyone always wins, even when you can't see how that's possible.

You still see your heart and me as separate from you. You all do. There are homeless billionaires sleeping on the streets all over the world, and still not one of you will believe this. Almost the entire world sees them as they see themselves, homeless and without money. You look at them and say, "But we know this is true, and the entire world agrees, so how can it not be?"

My initial thought is to say that you and the entire world have never been more wrong, but when I think of all the things you don't understand yet, this may not be completely true, either. This is not meant as an insult. You are on a journey, and all of your peers are on a journey as well, whether they are consciously aware of it or not. You are all in different places, taking your own unique journeys, and no one's journey has a final destination. In individual terms, no one is behind or ahead of anyone else, because everyone is in a perfect place for them at every moment. They are also in a perfect place for everyone else, but few of you can see this yet.

You chose a journey to authenticity, although of course you had some help with this decision. Everyone is on a journey to authenticity, but this only becomes a choice when, through awareness and understanding, it becomes a *conscious* journey. How you have lived most of your life, culminating with the time you spent in New York City, was necessary so that you could reach the level of awareness and understanding to make your journey to authenticity a conscious choice. You are right about being in your current situation to make your dreams come true and to bless yourself and the world. You are right about this happening so that you can finally take care of lifelong problems with money, self-esteem, and, mostly, your idea of your true worth, but there is a great deal more to this.

Your fear of what others may think of you is still there, and this time it came from a side of you that you didn't expect. Your true worth will be revealed to you when the thoughts, words, emotions, and actions of others don't own you anymore. You and I both know that the *you* who created the situation you're in is almost completely gone and has been for a while now, and yet, although you *absolutely know* this, you still fear those who will *erroneously* see you this way, now. You *know* they will all be wrong about who they see you as now, and yet you still allow their image of you to hurt you. Getting to a place of awareness and understanding at an even higher level than you have ever written about is your greatest gift here, and of course you are writing about it now. I know this is a huge challenge for you, but you are ready for this, now. If you were not ready for this, something you *were* ready for would be happening in its place. We won't let you lose.

(LS) That was incredible! I have been reading this over and over, and it is still hard for me to wrap my mind around the fact that this is happening. I have to admit that I see so much of myself in what you are saying to me. I know that you and I are supposed to be one and the same, but then how is it that you have said things to me that I have never thought of before? You are getting me to see myself in ways I have never seen before. Can you explain to me what is going on here? How can this be happening?

Also, I thought my greatest gift triggered by this situation was the energy and commitment that won't permit failure. Wouldn't this be a great thing for everyone? Your complete understanding of me knows I can't let this fail, now. Not only can I not let this fail now, but I can't change my mind and become a complete recluse. There was a short time when I thought I could actually just write alone forever and not care if anyone read anything or not, but because of where I am, because of what I've done, and more important, because of the messages delivered through feeling from you and my heart, I know that is not what my journey is about—at least not yet. Maybe once I take care of all that is already real in my heart, maybe then I will write for me only. I see this as possible at some point; I just don't see it anytime soon.

(My Soul) I know you think you are separate from me, but that is not true, and moreover, it is not even possible! Your heart has been my closest friend and favorite co-creator from before the beginning of life on any planet. Unlike me, your heart has a physical home inside your body. Your heart lives in two different worlds at the same time; not that it's alone in this endeavor, but let's take this one step at a time. Your heart is the ultimate in astral projection. There is no separation between you and your heart except for the separation the rest of you creates through the perception and belief that your heart is not you. This perceived and self-manufactured separation is not real, but your response to it makes it *your* reality.

Your heart and I are not only forever with you; we forever *are* you. You see so much of yourself in my words because all of you is in all of them. You seem to be surprised that this is happening, but what is really happening is nothing like you think. If what you call channeling is connecting to someone or something that is outside of you, then you have never channeled, and neither has anyone else. There is no outside of you. Everything that you call dead or alive, material or non-physical: none of this is separate from you. What you call "channeling" me is no different than your left leg channeling your right.

(LS) My God! I have never thought of it this way before. I'm very happy I started this conversation. I just submitted a partial manuscript to my writing coach; twenty-three thousand words, and a large part of it was about how everyone with a heartbeat is a channeler.

(My Soul) We have to be careful here, for much hinges on your definition of channeling. It doesn't matter to me what you call it, so long as you understand what is truly happening. Some in the physical world would see you as channeling me, but I know it's not that way at all. Your conversation with me is really your conversation with that part of *you* that you do not relate to. Most of you still doesn't consciously relate to me, at all. Among those of you who can describe me perfectly, most still don't believe their descriptions. I know this because I am just as much a part of them as I am a part of you.

(LS) Do I believe my description of you?

(My Soul) You have so much more to go. In relative terms, your awareness and understanding are at fairly high levels, but you don't yet live on the level of your awareness. You don't completely believe your description of me, but no one that you still see as outside of you does, either. You should be proud of the progress that you have made, but with the understanding that there is much more for you to look forward to.

(LS) Well, at least you're honest. You are certainly not so good for my ego.

(My Soul) As the higher, more authentic part of you, I say, "Thank you" to that.

(LS) Is that your version of a joke?

(My Soul) No, that is my version of the truth.

(LS) Hopefully, it will soon be mine, too.

(My Soul) I want to get back to your questions here.

There is only one reason for everything. Every event and circumstance has the "soul" purpose for you of seeing more clearly who you already are. Everything that happens is designed to make you grow in an unlimited number of ways. Your greatest challenge is whether you trust this and whether you can recognize at least one way to grow.

Nothing happens without the intention of your realization. Most of you would understand this as meaning that everything is meant to make you grow. It is not uncommon that what you see as most important in your life is not what I see as most important, although your understanding and awareness of your purpose have enhanced your vision tremendously in this arena. The energy and commitment to take care of what you say you *need* to take care of is a crucial part of your journey, but you are making it more than it is.

(LS) Do you not think I need to make right what I've done?

(My Soul) I know you don't need to do anything. We would all much prefer that you *choose* to make it right, as you say, if that is what makes you happy. I know this is where your heart is, and so I have no doubt that you will do it, but it is not right or wrong to take care of this or not; it is simply your choice.

(LS) I can't see a scenario in which the decision *not* to take care of this would be okay. Can you clarify this for me?

(My Soul) I was hoping you were going to ask me this.

(LS) You can't fool me that easily. There was never a moment you didn't know that question was coming; there was no hope involved.

(My Soul) Touché!

(LS) I can't imagine what your answer will be, but I'm very much looking forward to it.

(My Soul) You have personal experience with this. You know that giving anyone money is not what is best for them. You have been thinking about this as it relates to *your* journey, and that is good, but now think of how it relates to everyone else's journey. What will make them all grow more, handing them money they have not worked for, or making their own life and security?

(LS) I get that. I really do, but I was entrusted with their security, and I could not have done a worse job. I was trusted to carry out the desires of people I love, and I not only accepted this responsibility but was paid for it, as well. I have felt like a piece of garbage for a long time about this. You have made me feel much better, and I understand it more now than I ever believed I would, but that doesn't make what I did right. Regardless of what anyone thinks or says, if I am one hundred and six and have not taken care of this yet and I am still breathing, I will still be working on it.

(My Soul) Have you not yet come to a place where you understand that the only time it is beneficial to be in charge of anyone's security is during the time that you are teaching them how to be in charge of their own? I completely understand that you want to take care of this, and I'm not trying to tell you not to. I just want you to see that this is a selfish thing. This is all about you, and it is all for you. Fixing this the way you want to fix it is not restoring anyone's life but your own.

Again, I'm not telling you not to do this. I just want you to see the truth. I would not want to play a role in taking such a strong and authentic desire from you, nor would I wish to rob the universe of its expansion because of it, for it would go against everything me, your heart, and God believe in.

(LS) I guess I have been so blinded by the overwhelming desire to fix this that I never saw it that way. I can't believe how much you have opened my eyes. I would never have known how blind I have been. I can see the truth much more clearly, and still I am going to take care of this because it is what I see as the right thing to do. I was trusted to do a job by people I love and who also love me, and I'm going to complete the job I was trusted with successfully. I don't see it as my place to judge their "will."

(My Soul) I know this is super-important to you, and I

believe you should do what your heart says to do. Every sincere, authentic desire is nourishment that our universe thrives on, so why would I get in the way of such progress? I have no interest in whether you "take care" of this òr not. As far as I'm concerned, it has already been taken care of. You see, you and your peers will judge each other based upon what you do, and I know who you are independent of what you do. I would certainly not want you to judge or question anyone's decisions, opinions, or actions.

(LS) You make it sound as if there is no moral issue here, and that the only valid reason for making my decision is what is in my heart. What about my character?

(My Soul) Do you have a problem with your character? Do you not know who you are? If you know who you are, how can there be a moral issue?

(LS) No, I don't have a problem with my character, but I think I would have one if I just let this go. If I let this go, everyone would think I don't care, and I want people to know the truth. Is that so bad?

(My Soul) It's not bad to want people to know the truth, but it will be a much brighter day for you when you don't *need* them to. To the degree that you *need* anyone to see you in a particular way, whether it is true or not, they own you. You are on a journey to authenticity, and you are still hiding from the truth. Make whatever decision you want to make, but make it in complete awareness of the truth.

(LS) Wow! You are incredible! I can hardly believe this. Thank you.

(My Soul) Have you forgotten that you are both of us, or do you always compliment yourself and then show yourself appreciation for doing so?

(LS) You're a comedian, too?

(My Soul) It would not be possible for one of us to be and not the other, so I'm just making you feel at home.

(LS) You said there are homeless billionaires all over the world, but you mean that they are wealthy in ways that don't include money, right?

(My Soul) No, they are wealthy in all ways, including money, of course.

(LS) How can this be? It is pretty clear that they have no money or they wouldn't be sleeping on the street.

(My Soul) Evidently it is not all that clear. They, as well as you, have mistaken their financial lack for a lack of another kind.

(LS) That sounds great, but if I'm sleeping on the streets, how does that put a roof over my head or get me my next meal?

(My Soul) At your stage of development, it may not change your physical circumstances immediately, although it certainly could, but that doesn't change the fact that all of you are wealthy in every way, including financially.

(LS) Okay, you are not making any sense at all. Sounds like you have completely lost your mind.

(My Soul) Well, thinking isn't working too well for any of you, so that's probably a good thing.

(LS) Come on, if you're serious about this, explain it to me.

(My Soul) Okay, let's start out with something simple, but using the same concept. Let's say you decide you want to make some pancakes, but you notice that you don't have any milk in the refrigerator or anywhere else in the house. This doesn't mean you "don't have" milk. Your milk is being held in another place for you, and there is a different process for claiming what is yours. You grab your car keys, get in your car, drive to the store, take the milk off the shelf, hand the cashier some piece of paper with a deceased notable on it, and you drive home with "your" milk and make some pancakes. You would say, "If the milk were in my refrigerator, it would be considered mine; but if I have to go to the store and get it, or buy it, it's not mine until I pay for it," and this is just not true. Everything is yours; there is just a different set of steps and possibly a longer process if it is not what you call "yours."

(LS) But wait a minute—I can't drink the milk or make the pancakes without paying for it first, so how can it be mine until I pay for it?

(My Soul) If the milk were in your refrigerator right now, you also could not drink it or make pancakes until you opened the refrigerator. Does this make the milk not yours, as well?

Look, I'm not trying to make a joke out of this. Everything is yours right now, and the process for claiming it depends on where you are in relation to what is yours at this moment.

(LS) Then, if I'm homeless, and I want a mansion and a yacht, you're saying that they're already mine and all I have to do is go through the process of acquiring the money or resources to claim them?

(My Soul) Yes, exactly! Along with a few other steps, as well.

(LS) This is not really true; this is just your way of looking at it.

(My Soul) Half right. This is my way of looking at it, and it absolutely is true.

(LS) First of all, this is not easy for anyone and nearly impossible for a homeless person, and second, you just made this up.

(My Soul) The number of homeless people who have "become" wealthy, in your terms, would be almost as shocking to you as this concept, and there is one sitting in your chair, right now. I did make it up, and that doesn't make it untrue. It is only untrue for those who don't believe in it. The only reason why "it's yours after you pay for it" is true for so many people is because someone made it up, and almost everyone believed it.

(LS) Okay, so why would choosing your truth that everything is ours now be better than choosing the universally accepted truth that everything is ours after we pay for it?

(My Soul) Such a great question. There are an unlimited number of ways to look at everything, and these are only two, but you get to choose how you want to see this. Why not choose an empowering perspective? The reason you have not done so in the past is because you think there is only one truth. There are an unlimited number of truthful ways to see everything. Is this not the premise that all your writing is based upon?

(LS) Yes, it is. I write about seeing the truth in a way that empowers people; I just never heard it explained that way.

(My Soul) And as well as you've been doing, you're doing even better now.

(LS) Because of you?

(My Soul) No, because of *you*.

(LS) Don't you mean "us?"

(My Soul) Us, me, we, you—it's all the same.

YOU'RE IN A RELATIONSHIP WITH EVERYTHING THAT HAPPENS TO YOU

(LS) I WANT to ask you about something that I really thought I was completely over, but this new situation has made me aware that I am not.

(My Soul) You do really well with worry, except for situations that you created. Do you want to take a guess at why?

(LS) I guess I'm supposed to understand how you knew I was talking about worry. You're so right. I don't worry about anything unless I did it, and it's even worse if what I did has hurt someone else. I think it's because I feel responsible for hurting someone, and I feel their pain.

(My Soul) Sorry, but not even close. You don't worry about the things that you did. You worry about how you are seen. If you do something that was completely your fault and no one sees it as being your fault, you don't worry at all.

(LS) You make it sound like I don't care about anyone but me, and that's not true.

(My Soul) Do you see what I mean? You are now worried about how I see you. I never said you don't care about anyone but you. I know exactly who you are, and I don't need to hear you say or see you do something to confirm it; but you still need to hear and see it from others, including me, evidently.

You think that worry means you care, and worry never means you care. Worry always means you fear what is not there.

(LS) I wish I had started this when I was five. It would have saved me a truckload of pain.

(My Soul) It would not have saved you anything to start this earlier. What has already happened was the best that could have happened. I know you know this because I've told you so many times in so many ways, and you have not only gotten the message, but you agree, as well. Also, you did try this in the past, and you didn't connect.

(LS) If you already know what questions I'm going to ask before I ask them and you know what I know and what I don't, then why don't you just write the rest of this conversation by yourself?

(My Soul) I am.

(LS) I thought I was writing it.

(My Soul) You are.

(LS) Ahhhh...we are both the same person, right?

(My Soul) We are both the same, but I'm not sure I would say *person.*

(LS) Okay, not going to even touch that one.

(My Soul) As you wish.

(LS) How do we end worry for good?

(My Soul) I'm going to try to explain this in a way that you can relate to best. Do you know what it's like to be in a relationship where you love someone unconditionally?

(LS) You know I do.

(My Soul) Okay, now everything that happens in *your* life happens relative to *you*—would you agree with this?

(LS) Yes, I get that.

(My Soul) Just like the person whom you love, everything that happens *relative* to you in your life is also a *relationship*. If you don't like things about the person you love, more things that you don't like will show up. And when you love everything about the person you love, more things you love will show up. Does this make sense to you?

(LS) Yes, and I see how this is *relative*, but I'm not sure how this is *relevant*.

(My Soul) Well, whether you know it or not, you are in a relationship with every event and circumstance in your life. If you don't unconditionally love the events and circumstances that have already taken place in your life, it won't matter how many problems you "fix," because new problems will be lining up before you ever fix the first one. As long as you see your life, your current situation, as a problem to fix, more problems are on the way.

You see, your vision of the present moment is the equivalent of re-ordering how you see the *now*. You don't have to know *how* problems will stop coming, or even how your current problem will disappear. Your *opportunity* is to see them differently. And the moment you see them differently, they're already gone. The phrase, "Love conquers all," is not just a cliché; it is real. Every moment is an opportunity to love, and every opportunity to love is what you call a miracle.

(LS) That sounds great, but how do you love something that is painful and hurts not only you, but people you love, as well?

(My Soul) Didn't I answer this already?

(LS) I didn't ask it in the same way.

(My Soul) Should I give you the same answer in a different way? You are the only one that you have hurt, and you only hurt because you have not grown up yet.

(LS) Come on, this is completely not fair.

(My Soul) You asked for the journey to authenticity. Would you rather I lie?

(LS) I want the truth, but that is a little harsh, don't you think?

(My Soul) If your ego needs a massage, it has come to the wrong spa.

(LS) No, no, I'm trying really hard to give my ego a *message*, not a massage.

(My Soul) And you are doing a great job of getting that message across. You have come a long way, but please understand where you are and where you are going.

(LS) Was that your version of a compliment?

(My Soul) You really have come a long way, and you need to see the truth about everything.

(LS) Okay, I know you have said that I am the only one I have hurt, but no one I know would agree with that, and certainly none of those who are affected.

(My Soul) So, what everyone believes is still more important to you than the truth?

(LS) Although I've never thought about it the way you put it, I completely get what you're saying, but how do I get everyone else to see the truth?

(My Soul) The only problem you have is wrapped up in that one question.

(LS) How can it be wrong for everyone to see the truth?

(My Soul) It's not, but you must lead the way, and you are resisting seeing the truth about you. People seeing the truth is not the problem; the problem is your *need*, your *insistence* to have that happen. You have learned to love people unconditionally. You are very good at it. Now it is time for you to learn how to love all of your present moments unconditionally, with all of their truths. You are dealing with maybe the most difficult situation of your entire life, in your terms, and you have found many blessings. Do you see what this "horrible" situation has already done *for* you?

(LS) I do see that. I really do. The evolution of my relationship with you is, by far, my greatest gift ever. I never expected it to happen. I didn't think it was possible to be so real. I started to write to you for the sole purpose of making me feel better about what I've done, and it has become a "soul" purpose, instead. I just wanted to gain some clarity in my situation. I have never been more excited about anything in my life. I can't believe it took me so long to find you. I have many more questions I want to ask you.

(My Soul) You think our relationship started on the day we started writing to each other, but this relationship has no beginning time. This has been going on much longer than your awareness of anything. You have even been communicating with me consciously for longer than you think.

(LS) This may be so, but I never thought you would answer me back in words.

(My Soul) You never tried until three days ago.

(LS) I never thought to try until I started to do "The Work," imagining its founder and creator, Byron Katie, as the one answering my questions—or more appropriately, as the one asking me the right questions. I was just trying to learn how not to worry about my situation when all of a sudden she came alive and started telling me things I never heard before. It was such a shocking experience. Here is a person who is still alive, someone who has no "conscious" idea that I even exist, and yet she gave me advice directly! Can you tell me what this was and how it happened?

(My Soul) Sure. This is not the first time this has happened for you. You are so loved—and not just you, but all of you are so loved. All of you are being helped, and not just by those who have "died," in your terms. You are all being helped by each other all the time. Those who say they hate you also love you, only they are way too disconnected to be consciously aware of it. You have a friend who has gotten quite frustrated with you, consciously, but she loves you so much that she has found someone for you to love in a way that you could not love her. You are a perfect match in every way, while also keeping you on track toward your ultimate realization, ultimate growth. Asking your friend about this will not help. Your friend has no conscious awareness of it. This new person in your life is perfect for your journey to authenticity, just as you are for hers, but will you both listen to my messages? I know you are aware of all the synchronicities, and it is your awareness of our mission for you that makes this possible for you.

Your awareness has gone beyond the synchronicity of dates, names, and numbers to an understanding of their meaning and their role in your ultimate mission. Every cell in your body has a soul of its own, and these cells are connected even when the rest of you is not. You all have the power to connect to anyone you want at any time. Your connection to Byron Katie was real, just as your connection to me is real. Neither your friend nor Byron Katie need to be consciously aware of what they have done for you.

Even those who don't believe they can do such a thing are doing it all the time. The fact that not everyone reads the right signs makes this invisible to many people. You have been aware enough to see and notice what's happening. You know that all things lead to a forever higher version of your personality; therefore it's easier for you to make the choices that are in line with our mission for your journey. Your peers may not see your choices as right most of the time, but they don't understand your journey.

What you and those in your life see as your greatest failures and most destructive decisions, we know to be the greatest and most valuable events of your life. These were planned and designed to be your greatest gifts, but these gifts only open to the appropriate response. These gifts only open to actions of love, and love is so much more than most people think. Actions of belief, faith, and knowing are all a part of love. These are all things you have written about. Actions that say to the universe, "I believe anything is possible." Your actions in the face of the most challenging experience of your life could be so much better, but you have never thrown in the towel. It's not in you; you're not the type. When your heart is set on something, you never let it go unless and until your heart changes; and when your heart changes, your desire changes. This is not giving up. We eventually learn that there are things we really don't want.

No one knows you better than I do. We are helping you peel back and remove each destructive layer of your ego, one small section at a time. You have told people that you are done with ego. You have conquered a lot, but you have much further to go than you think. There are things you still don't see, or you don't want to see, yet. There is a part of you that wants to see the truth in everything, but the part of you that still fears the truth pretends it is not there. Also, others not seeing your decisions as right or appropriate is part of your journey when it happens that way. This is part of the process of growing out of the need to be seen in a specific way.

When you finally learn and understand the language I speak, you will know as I do that every decision you've ever made, was the most valuable decision you could have made for you and everyone else at that time. Those decisions that you say, "hurt you and many others," are among the most valuable and yet unopened gifts, and these are not only gifts to you, but they are also gifts to whoever else you say you hurt.

Understanding the language of feeling is like the scissors that cut the ribbon and the wrapping paper of your greatest gifts. But until you have this understanding, those gifts will be seen erroneously as the most destructive events and decisions you've ever made in your life.

So, while everyone else is either angry at you or feeling sorry for you, I am the kindred spirit who knows the absolute truth, and to you I say *congratulations!* Your graduation present is on the way.

(LS) That is awesome, but also a little confusing.

(My Soul) Did you ever get this feeling inside that you wish you had the power to fix something that happened—or maybe this feeling was so strong that you knew you would fix it even though you had no idea where to start? You thought, "How can I have done this?" or, "I can't believe someone did this to me!" and yet, nothing wrong was ever done; in fact, everything was done perfectly.

There is a scientific formula for determining whether everything was done perfectly, and that formula is this: It happened! All you ever need to know about events and decisions being right is that, if it happened, it must be the best possible thing for your ultimate realization. Some of us see this "realization" as growth, enlightenment, or becoming, but the truth is, we have already grown all we will ever grow. We are—right now—as enlightened as we will ever be, and there is nothing we can possibly become that we aren't already. We simply have not *realized* this yet, which means we have not yet become aware of it, or displayed it as real.

(LS) Ahh…Touché. You certainly said more than I expected you to say.

COMMITMENT FROM THE HEART

(LS) HOW CAN I help people without knowing I'm helping them?

(My Soul) You already do. You just authentically love with no conditions, and the rest just happens. Love is the most powerful force in the universe, and it is a moment-by-moment choice. You are so much more powerful than you think you are—all of you are—but many times you choose fear, and in doing so, you relinquish your power—the part you're aware of, at least.

(LS) You know what my greatest challenge is here, and I really believe I'm way too smart to be in this situation. You have taught me how to rise above it. I thought I was good at seeing things in more empowering ways, but you have shown me how little I knew.

(My Soul) On the contrary, I have shown you how much you have always known.

(LS) Wow! Touché!

Okay, I know I don't have to fix this, or anything, but as you know all too well, that is where my heart already is. How do I get there? How do I get to where my heart is, now? Can you tell me what I've been doing wrong, why I'm not there already? I know that I start and stop and don't follow through, but this is something I want to accomplish in as short a time as possible, because I don't know if I have five years or the next second.

(My Soul) You know exactly how to get to where your heart is right now, and you've been doing it at least twice a day, but when you're not paying attention, you still disconnect. You've been getting closer and closer to living this way. You are there now as you type the words you are typing in this very moment. There are not many who understand this better than you do. You insist on asking me to give you answers you already have. You are the one who writes about "level of commitment." Where is your level of commitment in handling this, right now? You can't commit on Monday, take a day off on Tuesday, and expect to get where you say you want to go.

(LS) I don't take any days off, and why do you speak as if I don't know what I want here? I see what I want as pretty clear, with no mixed signals.

(My Soul) If you were clear, you would never ask how to get to where your heart is. Writing every day, alone—do you call this committing at the highest level to accomplish something that not many would even believe is possible? When was the last time you committed at your highest possible level to taking care of what you still call your "problem?" Accomplishing what you want to accomplish will take becoming someone you have never come close to becoming, and you have been fooling yourself for a long time about your level of commitment.

In regard to what you say you want to accomplish, you are not committing yourself. On your adventure to authenticity, you are not only hiding from others, you are also hiding from yourself. You are not being truthful with yourself, and this you must do before you can accomplish even a fraction of what you now "hope" to. What you hope to accomplish, but have not yet committed to accomplish, takes a level of discipline that you have not yet reached, even in your most disciplined years. If you are really serious about this, you need to come clean to "you." I'm not taking away what you have done, for you have come a long way, but what you say you want and what you are doing about it have never been further apart. The progress you have made was made by moving toward your heart, even if timidly at times. You're not going to get to where you want to go by just writing every day, regardless of how many hours you put in.

(LS) Oh, you are so right! What have I been thinking?

(My Soul) I will let you in on a little secret. You will *never* get what you want for you unless "we" get what "we" want for you. Do you understand this? Align your dreams for you with our dreams for you and what happens from there you will see as magic; what we will see is you connecting the dots, you finally putting it all together.

(LS) I can't believe this! This is amazing! Where is this coming from? Wait—don't answer that, yet. I want to finish this first.

Okay, so what exactly do I do from here to fix what I have done? What steps do I take? Can you help me with the details?

(My Soul) Come on, you know better than to ask me that. Helping you in that way defeats my purpose for you; it would be no different than me handing you the money needed to fix what you still say is broken. Doesn't that sound familiar to you? Don't you see how giving you the exact steps, or worse, handing you the money, would be robbing you of your true identity? When I question you about why you want to *fix* the *blessing* that started this conversation, it's not because I don't think you should *act* on it, I wanted to see how you see your situation. I still stand by what I said: "There is nothing to fix."

(LS) Wait a second! If you and I are one, wouldn't you helping me be me helping me, as well? I know that. I understand it, now. What's wrong with that?

(My Soul) I am helping you. I am helping you always to

become the highest version of you, and I am doing this in every moment.

(LS) I think I get that, and I know you've explained this before, but can you explain it again for me?

(My Soul) Sure. This thing you want to take care of is something that you have been dealing with and consciously aware of for many months now, right?

(LS) Yes, that's true.

(My Soul) So, would you really want it to be magically taken care of for you right now, knowing that if it were, you would have to go all the way back to who you were before this problem, or at least back to who you were before your awareness of it?

(LS) Whew. I am completely drenched in tears. Now, I remember when my journey to authenticity became a conscious decision. Somehow, you just triggered that memory. You are amazing. Thank you. Thank you!

It happened less than a year before the time I'm writing this. I know I have a lot further to go, but now I can see clearly how far I've come in a very short time. I can see clearly *all* the things I *never* would have done if I hadn't received such a blessing. So, it's true that everything really is *for* us?

(My Soul) You have been telling me and everyone else that you know this.

(LS) I know, and I do know this from many other experiences, as well, but I have been saying that this is the worst situation I have ever experienced in my life, and now you have gotten me to see the truth. You have made me experience a huge part of what I write about. I no longer just profess the truth; I now *know* it firsthand, experientially. Although at times I am still scared to death about whether I will actually fix this situation or not, I would not want it to be fixed *for* me. I would not want to be robbed of who I am.

I have literally gone from "This is the worst thing that has ever happened to me" to "This is the greatest, most significant event of my life." What it has done for me, even before this conversation with you, is not something I can easily explain. My nightmare has truly become my miracle. Although I have written about this, you have given me a new set of glasses to see through, glasses that I believe can see through walls.

(My Soul) The glasses you say I gave you were created so that one could see through something much thicker than any walls; they see through all of your fears. I would say I'm happy knowing you can see much more clearly now, but I was happier than I ever could be even before your newfound vision, because I always knew that your next stage of realization was imminent. Can you also see, now, how much better this is for everyone involved than if everything had gone as planned in earthly terms?

(LS) I certainly see how it potentially can be, for my kids, anyway. I just can't see how any of this would help my sister. What if everyone involved is so angry about this that they never read this conversation or never learn even part of what I have learned from this? How can they grow if they can't get past the anger and pain of this?

(My Soul) Their response to what happens in their lives is *their* journey; all you can do is present them with the gift. You have known for a long time to trust this process; if you hadn't, you would not be ready to understand me and this conversation would not have gone very far, if it had started at all, at least not now. In your world, when you give someone a present, it is up to them whether they choose to open it. This is no different. You clearly trust the process for you, and as I said before, you must learn to trust the process for everyone else, as well, even in their anger with you.

(LS) I do trust the process for everyone else. I *know* it works. This has been such an exciting day for me. I feel an incredible shift because of what we did today. Every day, I have been feeling better, but today really did it for me. The key was when you asked me if my problem could be magically fixed right now, would I be willing to go back to who I was before I did this. Something happened at that moment. I felt, and I still feel, different about this than I ever have before. I can't wait to wake up tomorrow and see if I still feel the same. Such a great feeling, such an amazing revelation!

Although I do trust the process for everyone, it's not easy to keep quiet when I clearly see what someone should be doing. At the same time, the answer is not always something you can just say during a normal conversation. Eventually, I would love to see my kids understand your language of feeling and synchronicity—and, of course, ultimately to act on it. What I have learned from you through feeling and synchronicity is something I would love to help the entire world see, and not just see, but *live*, too.

(My Soul) You have already started to do it. Don't you see that?

(LS) Yes, I have, but it's not nearly enough to make an impact on the world.

(My Soul) You would be shocked at how even just smiling at one person affects the entire universe, from a blade of grass to the sand, the ocean, the sun, the moon, the stars, and everything else. There is no separation between you and anyone, or between you and anything.

DIVORCE FEAR IN YOUR ACTIONS

(LS) HOW DO I help more people and at the same time take care of the mess I've got myself and those I love into?

(My Soul) After yesterday, you are still calling this a mess?

(LS) Yesterday was incredible. You somehow triggered a shift in me, but everyone in my world will see this as the worst thing I've ever done, so the word *mess* just seems appropriate here.

(My Soul) From where I stand, what you have done is not only perfect for everyone directly affected, but depending on what you do from here, it has the potential to change the world. Do you see this, and do you see how it depends on what you choose now and your moment-to-moment choices from here on?

(LS) Yes, I do, and I'm very excited about that.

(My Soul) Your response to your heart's and my communications to you have taken you to a great place. Now, what you still vacillate between calling the greatest, most significant event in your life and your biggest mess has unlimited, future possible meanings. Whether you are aware of it or not, you are deciding what these future meanings will be in every one of your present moments. This is all your choice, but it will remain an "every-right-now" choice. As we talk about what you may choose in the future, synchronicity is working all the time.

Your youngest daughter just called about three hours ago, just a few minutes before we started this part of the conversation. You accurately sensed that she was feeling a little down and gave her a motivational speech that she needed to hear. Do you remember?

(LS) Are you stalking me, now?

(My Soul) I will take that as a "yes." You also found a motivational video that contained the exact words you were thinking would help her, and you emailed it to her. Her phone call, your motivational speech, and the video you found for "her" were just as much for you as they were for her. You both needed something, and you provided it for each other. She provided the phone call and the sentiment, which triggered your motivational speech and the video you quickly found, both of which were meant for both of you. This is synchronicity! I know you became aware that the motivational speech was not just for your daughter in the moment you started speaking, and of course, you very much connected with the video regarding your life right now.

(LS) Oh, my God! I can't believe this! Every day has been a miracle since I found you.

(My Soul) Every one of your days has been what you call a miracle; you are just starting to realize it, now.

Let's get back to your question. We took a little detour, a valuable one, but a detour nonetheless. You wanted to know how to affect more people in a positive way, and at the same time "fix" the greatest thing that has ever happened for you. Did I get that right?

(LS) Touché, wise guy.

(My Soul) Do you think I did not notice that recently in this conversation, you changed your initials from those of your personal name to the initials of "Love Story?"

(LS) Do you think it's a good idea to reveal this conversation? This has been the most amazing thing that has ever happened to me. This is the most valuable conversation I have ever experienced, but will it really have any value to anyone else?

(My Soul) Thanks for the compliment, but remember, you are the only one with an ego here. Why do you insist on asking me questions to which you already know the answers? You know what the conversation has already done for you, so how can it possibly not have value to a world as hungry for answers as you are?

You know exactly what to do. Now stop asking me about this and go do it, if you really want what you say you want.

(LS) My Soul has anger issues?

(My Soul) You can joke around about this all you want, but I won't answer the same questions asked in different ways just because you're too afraid to follow through. You're great at starting; you've had a lot of practice with that. You don't want me to tell you how many times you've started and not followed through. I'll save that for when you have a better relationship with your ego, or better yet, none at all.

(LS) I never thought my Soul would ever be this mean to me.

(My Soul) I'm sorry, but this is clearly still a part of love that "Love Story" does not get, yet. Look, I just want you to be honest with yourself and whoever else you share your plans with. Every part of you speaks of these grand desires you appear to have, while your actions speak of nearly constant fear. One of your questions somewhere in here was about why you don't follow through, and your answer lies in the relationship your actions still have with fear. Your actions need to divorce fear. No worries, no attorney needed this time. Fear gets to keep everything it brought into the relationship, and you get me back.

(LS) Is that really it—what's been keeping me from following through?

(My Soul) Absolutely, and you know exactly what to do, so just go do it.

(LS) What do you mean, I get "you" back?

(My Soul) Neither your heart, nor I, can be found in fear. We don't even know what it really is; we just know it's not real. We see fear as you watching a cartoon with monsters that you believe can somehow jump through the TV, become real, and kill you.

(LS) Ha-ha-ha! Are you serious about that?

(My Soul) Absolutely! It is not possible for us to experience anything that is not real; therefore, in order for us to describe fear, we are forced to make up something nonexistent, the most artificial thing we can think of. How did I do?

(LS) Oh, my God! You've gotta be kidding me! Well, it's very real to us.

(My Soul) "Well," I would suggest your actions, along with the rest of you, be a lot more like us and a lot less like all of you. You have written about this many times, and you do it really well when you do it, but you either stop on your own or you let something that's not real derail you.

(LS) What do you mean by that? Are you talking about fear again?

(My Soul) Very good, but do you know where you get it from, and do you know how you're going to get rid of it?

(LS) I have an idea where it comes from. At times, when someone says something or something happens, it gets triggered in me. The confusing thing for me is that there are times when those same things happen and I experience no fear and no worry.

(My Soul) This is because events and words have nothing to do with fear; they are merely events and words. You conveniently forgot to mention your favorite cartoon, *Disapproval*. Again, please understand, we see all of your fears as cartoons, and it would benefit you to see the characters in your "Fear" production" as cartoons, too, with all of their disapproving reactions. See everyone in your artificial production as a distorted caricature. This would surely change the way you feel about the situation.

(LS) Sorry, but it took me about five minutes to peel myself off the floor. I *love* that.

Except for one thing. It feels like I'm being disrespectful to everyone affected by it.

(My Soul) You are on an adventure to authenticity and still pretending you don't know the truth. You are now thinking of everyone's reactions and that you are making a mockery of "hurting them," and, of course, you are uncomfortable with them seeing it this way, seeing "you" this way, correct?

(LS) Yes, exactly. It is a clear sign of disrespect!

(My Soul) Nothing can be further from the truth, but do you see what happens? You allow the *possible* reactions of others, along with their *perceived* disapproval of you, to decide what is right, and you agree with them. You agree with them even knowing that they can't see the truth from where they stand and that only you can. You have said that if you are a hundred and six years old, still breathing, and this has not been taken care of yet, you will still be working on it, and you are worried about someone thinking you are making a joke of this?

There is only one worry here, and that is the worry of being seen as a loser who doesn't care what he has done to those he loves.

(LS) Wow! You are really taking brutal honesty to a new level.

Even though at times it hurts, I really do want the truth.

(My Soul) I know you do; this would not be happening if you didn't want the truth. The question of *who* you are need only be answered by you. Although you may understand it, you cannot be responsible for what anyone else thinks. You can only be responsible for the truth.

(LS) Yes, I get that, but you said that there are an unlimited number of ways of seeing the truth, right?

(My Soul) Yes, that's right, and you can choose what you want your truth to be. So, you can customize your own truth and claim it, *realize* it. Make it real and display it as such.

(LS) Such as in my current situation; the truth can be what everyone sees and believes, or I can make it into something I choose by aligning my desires with yours. Did I get that right?

(My Soul) That is perfect!

You get to choose what the truth means, and in so doing, you get to change the truth. As you have just learned, you can take something that happened and accept it as what everyone sees, at face value, or convert it to what you choose by listening to what we are saying to you and lining up with our purpose for you. In your case, a disaster becomes a blessing, and as I said to you before, what you do from here will determine how much of a blessing it will be, not only to you and those you say are affected, but possibly the entire world if you ever make that choice.

(LS) I really think I get most of that except the last part. So, you and I, doing what we do here every day—isn't that part of the choice you are saying I have not yet made?

(My Soul) Yes, of course, it is, and that's great, but this part alone will not take you where every part of you has been saying you want to go.

(LS) Ahh...so you are nudging me higher?

(My Soul) Forever! I love my mission, and I love you.

(LS) Did I just achieve loving myself, here?

(My Soul) Not fully, but you're moving in the right direction.

Your journey, or adventure to authenticity, as you have been calling it, is a journey away from fear and worry and to a place of love. You know exactly what to do; you have just been too afraid to do it, too afraid to continue doing it. Whenever you are

ready, just start and never look back. And for as long as you do, I
promise you, I will be right by your side.

I promise, you are more alone in a room full of people than
you are when you *think* you can't find a soul.

(LS) That is profound. I kind of wish I had written it.

(My Soul) You did!

(LS) Amazing! It is one thing to say, or even to believe, that
we are all one, but to know it through experience like this is
beyond what I ever could have imagined.

(My Soul) You have experienced this before, and you have
also been consciously aware of it. In your writing, it was not this
formal, so it may not have been so evident to you, but it was still
very clear. So many times you have pulled your car over to the
side of the road because you *felt* you had to write something—
no idea and no conscious thought, just a *feeling*. This is when we
do our best work.

(LS) When I was a kid playing basketball and running the
hills, those experiences I had—that was you?

(My Soul) Absolutely, and I'm impressed that you remember
me from that long ago.

(LS) You have always known that I did.

(My Soul) Such a beautiful thing when we have a great
connection. I better be careful about what I say. I don't want to
cause you any drama.

Do you remember from whom you heard the words "only
the truth matters?"

(LS) Yes, I know exactly who, and I always knew that was
supposed to happen. Every arrangement that my friend made
on that entire trip turned into a magical experience for me. The
people and the places. It was like it was from another world. It
was as if she was connected to God. I always knew I was not
alone. Just like now; such a comforting feeling.

(My Soul) "Like" it was from another world? "As if" she was connected to God?

(LS) Touché. Thank you.

(My Soul) Okay, I know you have to get this one out of your system, so go to the fast food place, but I will be ready as soon as you are ready to commit. You can always go to Squeezed Juice Bar tomorrow and get some cold-pressed organic juice. At the moment you definitely commit, then *I* move, too.

(LS) Ugh. Did you have to say that? Now, everyone thinks I'm a pig.

(My Soul) I didn't say what you order. Plus, only the truth matters, right?

(LS) Thank God for small favors, and the truth is not good, and you know it.

(My Soul) Well, you know how to change it. All you need to do is decide, and I will be there.

(LS) So, we were talking about other times in my life when I was aware you were there. The times I remember the most were certain times when I was playing basketball and I knew I couldn't do anything wrong. And running the hills when, at one point, I felt like I was being carried up. I wanted to talk to someone about these experiences back then, but I couldn't think of anyone who would take me seriously. These feelings were so incredible that I have been trying my whole life to get back there, and I have at times. It's like an athlete in the *zone*.

It feels like you and my heart have taken over my mind to move my body without thought.

I remember many years ago when we got a new TV. I was sitting with my kids in the family room of our first house. The Chicago Bulls were playing, and I was half-watching the game and half-reading the TV owner's manual, and if you ask anyone who knows me, that is a very dangerous thing. Call 911 before I have a chance to read any owner's manual, as something is surely about to burn down.

Anyway, after hitting many shots in a row, Michael Jordan hit another shot and ran back down court. Facing right into the camera, he shrugged his shoulders and mouthed the words, "It wasn't me." A few seconds later, one of my kids asked me why I was crying. I had tears in my eyes. I felt very emotional. I had never spoken about my experience to anyone, but I knew somehow that Michael Jordan had tapped into the same thing. I used the same three words, "It wasn't me," but only to myself. A few times when someone congratulated me for an "inhuman" game, I said to myself, "I guess I'm supposed to take credit for this, but it wasn't me."

❧

(LS) Before I left to get some food about three hours ago, you told me that when I was ready to commit, you would always be there. As I left, I felt this incredibly peaceful feeling. It didn't feel like it normally does. I wasn't walking, something was walking me and I wasn't moving any part of my body, I was being moved. This has happened to me before, but it's been a while. I always seem to somehow lose this after a while. I look forward to the day I never lose this again. Hopefully I'm not asking to die without knowing it.

It's been more than three hours, and you're still there. I'll let you know how I feel in the morning.

WHY DO YOU SHOW UP AT CERTAIN TIMES AND NOT OTHERS?

(MY SOUL) IT'S morning. How do you feel?

(LS) When I woke up, I felt sick form eating too much, but I've shrugged it off. I noticed you are back. Not just here, writing to me, but as the same peaceful feeling in my entire body.

(My Soul) Great, to everything, including feeling sick from eating too much.

Yes, I was with you during those times, and it was so beautiful. But those are not the only times I'm with you.

(LS) Okay, can you explain to me why you show up at certain times, and why at other times you just leave me hanging out to dry?

(My Soul) I don't leave you hanging anywhere. It is not my job to save you from what you don't want to happen. It is my mission to take you higher, make you more. It is my "soul" mission to get you to see who you have always been, and that doesn't happen by just handing you what you want.

I am always with all of you, but I respond to "unquestioned commands of knowing." Not one of you questions whether you can walk; you just *know* that you can, and so I show up and make it happen. But this, you will laugh at. This you will not see as a miracle, but it is just as much a miracle, in your terms, as everything else you call a miracle. Here it is: Your heart beats about 100,000 times a day and, of course, to you this is no big deal. However, if you received a FedEx delivery of $100,000 every day, you would be thanking God for finally recognizing your worth. You would see it as your greatest miracle, and we would see it as your greatest nightmare. You would say, "Now, I can really live." And we would say, "This would be the death of you."

(LS) I completely get it. I'm not sure I would have gotten it a year ago, but I believe I do, now. Can you elaborate on this for those who think we're both crazy, here?

(My Soul) Of course. You would all say that the $100,000 is the greatest gift ever, and we would say, "It kills all of our gifts to you." Love, faith, ambition, and drive would all take a long vacation. Along with your daily FedEx delivery would also be the delivery of perpetual adolescence. Who knows this better than you? You have had your own experiences with the "FedEx package" and life, and "I" have helped you choose a new path. However, you were ready for this, and as you know, not everyone is. Of course, the numbers were a lot smaller than what we're talking about, here.

You also know how this same thing is killing someone else, right now. Rewards that have not been earned are no match for true, authentic achievements, no matter how large or small. We assess every one of your circumstances and situations from the place of what it will make of you, from your perspective. You evaluate your circumstances and situations based upon who you can impress and how little you can do.

Do you understand this distinction and do you see the insanity in it?

(LS) Yes, I definitely do, but wouldn't you agree that I am not that way anymore? Don't you see that I have changed?

(My Soul) I do, and you have made remarkable progress, but it has been only a year, and your perceived resources are still diminished from your perspective. Let's see what you do when you're back on what you call "top" again.

(LS) What I call "top?"

(My Soul) Your top has been our bottom for you, and your bottom has been our top for you.

(LS) Was it really a good thing not to have a roof over my head?

(My Soul) If we had to choose between perpetual adolescence and homeless and closer to enlightenment, you know where our vote would be. Of course, we want you to have a roof over your head, but how you get there is more important to us. There will come a time when your "up" and our "up" will be one. Will that be at your next big success? Only time will tell, but why rush? You have forever, and when you get there will be perfect, no matter when that is. There is no need ever to worry. It is not possible to get any part of this wrong.

(LS) I hope no one gets bored with me saying "wow" again, but wow!

(My Soul) I think you'll be surprised at how well this will be received, and its reception would be so much better if you didn't care about it so much. Now, let's get back to where we were.

Most of you know that if you practice riding a bike for a few days, you will get it, so I show up more fully on the day you believe you will get it. It doesn't matter what *it* is, and the degree of difficulty has no influence on whether you can do something, or even on how long it will take. In reality, there is no degree of difficulty in anything. What you call "degree of difficulty" is completely your perception, your level of belief or knowing. Once you have all the information, everything is belief. When you believe something that no one else does, that is when others will see you as someone "out of this world." But you are not really out of your world; you are just operating outside others' beliefs.

Can you remember times when you were driving in your

car while you were reading something, or worse, texting? Can you remember a time when you were so involved in what you were reading or texting that, for a while, you were not even aware that you were still driving, and yet, when you finally looked up through the windshield, you were exactly in the middle of your lane and completely safe? Do you remember this happening more than once?

(LS) Yes, yes I do. I don't know how I went as far as I did, and I don't know how long I was driving like that, but it was always scary to me. What was it, and how did I do it?

(My Soul) You were not driving; I was.

(LS) What? Come on! Stop! Cops hate me as it is, so how am I supposed to explain that one? Can I be arrested if I can't produce my soul's license?

(My Soul) I'm not joking; this is *very* serious. In the instant you become *aware* that *you* have been driving, whether that is true or not, you will immediately go off the road or into another lane—and you can, what you call "die" instantly. This is only one reason why reading or texting while driving would be "so dangerous" to you, in your terms.

(LS) Oh! You were serious. I thought awareness was a good thing?

(My Soul) Awareness is a good thing when you are attempting something you have the ability to do consciously. Driving a car that does not drive itself while reading a book is not a good idea if you want to remain on earth. None of you are ready for this. You don't understand me, or even yourselves, well enough, yet.

(LS) How did the driving happen, then, even for the time it went on?

(My Soul) You can say that driving became somewhat of an involuntary activity, kind of like your heartbeat. Who do you think beats your heart?

(LS) This is incredible! Really?

(My Soul) It is, only don't try it with something that, when you disconnect, can change your life on earth in a way you don't currently want. Try it with a sport or while achieving anything in which you can be safe. I know that you have experienced this while driving, and that was a great way to get you to see what you are capable of.

(LS) Thank you! So, how do I use this capability safely in life?

(My Soul) We're getting there. Let's continue.

(LS) Okay, getting back to the question I said I would get back to: what happened last night when I thought I was finished writing and left my hotel to get something to eat?

(My Soul) You know firsthand who I am to you, and not only because of this conversation. What we are talking about every day is becoming increasingly more real to you. Your unquestioned knowing of who I am, combined with me telling you to "just commit and I will be with you," triggered what you felt when you left the hotel.

(LS) Yes, it was as if it wasn't me going to get the food. It felt like my feet didn't touch the ground, like I was being carried— just as I felt as a kid when I was running the hill.

(My Soul) Yes, all true; except now you know better than to say, "It wasn't me."

(LS) Yes, I know it is me, and I know it is us. My youngest daughter connects, or at least I know she has. How can I inspire others to feel this, to get to this place?

(My Soul) Everyone connects. I think what you mean is to connect consciously, to become aware that they are connecting. You are starting to get them there, now. The way to get them there completely is to make the commitment without starting over again.

(LS) Thank you, I will.

(My Soul) We'll see.

(LS) Thanks for the vote of confidence.

(My Soul) I completely believe in you, because I know exactly who you are. It is *you* who has had a problem with that—in the past, right?

When you really know who you are without question, everything becomes automatic, in your terms. Did you forget that everything you choose is already yours? Now, just go through the process of claiming it from where you are—if, of course, that is what you want. Don't try to force belief or knowing, just permit the energy to flow through focus, as you did last night and as you are doing right now.

(LS) Ahh. So beautiful. Thank you.

Can you explain to me what happened while I was running the hills as a young kid? It is extremely valuable for me to know how to get back there. I wasn't aware of any belief or knowing at that time. How did I trigger what happened there?

(My Soul) Let's start with your most current awakening of *me* and we can move backwards.

When you get to a place where you have no physical resources left and you keep going, doing whatever you can think of—you have just awakened *me*, and not only me. This conversation we are having arose when you were at the end of your physical resources.

(LS) I was in agony, searching for a way to end the suffering, and I wanted more than anything to find a way to fix the situation, from my perspective.

(My Soul) That is the key. You see, your choices were, for the most part, in line with my mission for you. Not once did you consider giving up, and because of this, we get to stretch what you see as possible. Unfortunately, in your situation, so many in your world would not even try. There would be no positive energy for us to work with.

(LS) What do you mean by "for the most part?"

(My Soul) We love the direction of your choices, and we know that, eventually, they will be *complete* choices. Complete in terms of follow through and commitment—but this will come when you're ready.

(LS) I know; I'm working on it.

(My Soul) There is no working on it. You either do it or you don't. You're moving in the direction of what you say you want, but you have not fully committed yet. You still believe your peers when they say it is possible to fail, and so you start and stop.

(LS) Well, it is possible to fail!

(My Soul) And that is the only reason why it is!

(LS) What is the only reason?

(My Soul) Your belief that it is possible to fail is the only ingredient that makes failure possible.

(LS) Is that really true? Many people say those words, but I personally don't know of anyone whose actions say that.

(My Soul) Beautifully stated.

(LS) You keep telling me that I am not completely committed. What do you mean by that? I have this seemingly monumental task in front of me to fix what I did, and I don't really know what to do first. Can you simplify this for me?

(My Soul) When you can live your entire life, or at least most of it, in the state of heart and mind that you began to experience last night when you went to get your food, everything you choose is yours, and no one can stop it from coming. What you call your "problem" would completely disappear right now if you knew everything was already perfect. When you not only understand this, but also experience it in your body—as you are right *now*!

(LS) Oh! You can feel that?

(My Soul) Absolutely. You are not separate from me.

(LS) So, this is the commitment you were talking about? Isn't there more to it than that? You had said that my actions didn't believe in me and that my actions were saying something different than my words, or something like that.

(My Soul) Exactly! Your actions did not trust you. Your actions were saying, "I don't believe in this, or you." Living in complete, unquestioned *knowing* means that you don't get disconnected by what happens. You completely *know* that, without your permission, what happens and what anyone says have no effect on where you are going. You know you must get there, and you have no fears or worries about anything.

(LS) Yes! I can feel exactly what you wrote.

Many times I have tried to get back this feeling from the experiences I had when I was much younger. And I have, often, but I have found that there is a huge difference when the feeling comes from focus rather than from manufacturing the feeling. Can you help me understand this better?

(My Soul) When the feeling arises from focusing on an authentic reason, you know why you feel the way you do; when you generate the feeling without a reason, you feel great but you don't know why. When you don't know why, anything can pull you off. But when you have concrete reasons, your emotional state is as solid as concrete. Knowing why you feel the way you do gives the feeling reason to stay; it gives it the purpose to become permanent; and reveals a simpler strategy for getting back there. More important still, when this feeling of extreme certainty comes from focusing on authentic, unquestioned knowing, it makes the feeling real, makes the belief real, or better yet, it makes the knowing real. Getting to the place of living your dreams, goals, or missions by focusing on "they're already done" will make more of your actions automatic—almost involuntary.

(LS) Thank you for not forgetting about explaining this process in more detail. What a great way to explain it, and what a great way to live.

(My Soul) Yes, living every moment of every day in the comfort of knowing the truth—*this* is true authenticity.

(LS) Incredible! I *love* it that we are having this conversation! I am so truly grateful that this is happening. I feel very blessed.

(My Soul) So, this worst thing that has ever happened to you—or however you want to refer to it—can you imagine life without it, now?

(LS) Oh, *no way!* It has become the greatest and most miraculous event of my life. I mean, I don't want to do anything like it again, and I do want to put things back together for my own sanity, but I love who I have become because of this. I love what I have learned, how I have grown because of it. Or, to be more accurate, I love how much I have realized and remembered about who I have always been. All of this is true now, and I haven't even accomplished what I thought was the most important part of it all, which I hope is still to come. Because of this experience, I see that I can literally choose, not only whether something is good or not, but even how good it is. I have learned that I can choose the level of blessings that come from *any* situation, regardless what it is.

This really is amazing.

(My Soul) I am so happy for you. You are finally starting to see the truth.

(LS) What you have said is beautiful. Life is beautiful. Everything is beautiful.

(My Soul) Do you see what we did here? We have enhanced your adventure to authenticity in a huge way. All we did was help you to see the truth. You now have much more to write about. Now you understand more fully the value of our language of feeling and synchronicity.

(LS) I do, I really do! Thank you.

LIVING IN COMPLETE,
UNQUESTIONED KNOWING

CAN WE GET back to my childhood experience of being carried up and down the hills, now?

(My Soul) Yes, yes, of course.

Think of that entire scenario in relation to all we've been talking about. At that moment during your childhood, your level of commitment to running faster was probably higher than anyone's and you were still just a little kid. You ran yourself to complete physical exhaustion. The muscles in your legs were not only twitching, but giving out on you, and yet you still did not stop.

Also, similar to how this conversation between us started, you were at the end of your physical resources that day on the hill, as well. Except, of course, you had a completely different set of resources. You mentioned that you could not recall a level of belief or knowing that could have triggered *me* while running your hill, but you are mistaken.

When you are at the end of your physical resources and it seems impossible to continue, but you still find a way to keep going, we see this as an extremely high level of faith, and we awaken to you in these moments. When I say, "the end of your resources," I mean from *your* perspective only, and I mean physically. You always have unlimited resources. *You are very often at the end of your resources*—again, from your perspective—and those in your world see this as a character flaw you have not yet corrected.

(LS) Don't you think it is? I see it that way, too.

(My Soul) I see it as the path you have chosen to your purpose.

(LS) But I know I did not intentionally choose it.

(My Soul) Can you be certain you did not choose it?

(LS) Are you saying that I chose this so I could realize who I have always been?

(My Soul) I believe it was you who said that.

(LS) I didn't have to hear the words; you were very clear. Yes, we both did.

(My Soul) Touché.

(LS) So sorry to switch gears here, but this is so important. Okay, so, my situation, now: was this something bad that I converted to good, or was it always meant to happen for a good reason?

(My Soul) You chose it, and when you did, you chose it from a place where realization was more important to you than peace on earth, or any other earthly desires, for that matter.

(LS) You know no one will believe this, right?

(My Soul) Are you talking about your situation, or theirs?

(LS) You always seem to know exactly what to say! I would love to have you in my car the next time I get pulled over. Although I'm not sure a mental hospital would be better than jail, there might be a little more to consider than which kind of crazy I prefer.

(My Soul) Are you having fun?

(LS) I could go on, but I will spare you.

So, it's true that where I end you begin?

(My Soul) Where you end, I begin; but only when you haven't given in. Do you get this?

(LS) Amazing!

(My Soul) By the way, I know it was a long time ago, but do you remember what it was like to achieve the level of commitment that you achieved as a child running the hills?

(LS) Of course.

(My Soul) Get to one quarter of that level now, in your current situation, and you'll "fix your problem," from your perspective, of course.

(LS) Really? That's it?

(My Soul) You think that's easy? It's not such a small order.

(LS) No, the opposite. To me, this is completely different. Granted, running the hills was not easy, but it was simple: run until you feel like you're dying, then call a cab to go half a block home, eat chicken au gratin, and collapse in bed at around one a.m. Then, keep doing it the next day and the next. It may take tons of determination and pain tolerance, but it's not rocket science.

(My Soul) So, you have forgotten how to think?

(LS) Of course not. It's just the magnitude of what I'm trying to do in the time I'm trying to do it; and the steps are not very clear. This makes me feel uneasy. As you, or anyone reading this conversation can see, I clearly have my moments of strength, and of course, my moments of weakness.

(My Soul) Do you really think that what you're going through right now is not normal?

(LS) I know it is normal; I just have to shake it off and keep moving.

(My Soul) That doesn't sound like rocket science to me.

(LS) Good one!

(My Soul) For you, right now, the steps are not supposed to be clear, this is part of your journey. You say this is not simple, but all you have to do is take one step, over and over again, until you get where you want to be. You don't need to ask any more questions about this. You know exactly what to do, and even how to get every answer you don't currently believe you have.

(LS) I know that, thank you. I just reread our conversations from the last two days. I know exactly what to do; it's all good.

(My Soul) I feel you. Welcome back. Do you understand the magnitude of what we did here?

(LS) I think I do.

(My Soul) Do you realize that *because of* what you used to call your worst nightmare ever, you now have the formula that could not only eliminate fear and worry for anyone, but take everyone closer to realization, while possibly making all of their dreams come true, as well? Also, your life is now the greatest example of it. Now, you can get anyone to do this because of what you call the worst thing you have ever done, as long as they are willing to follow your guidelines. Do you see how this fits your journey perfectly? Do you see how it fits our purpose for you?

(LS) I do see it, and I do understand all this. I have known for a long time how powerful our dialogue is, but this experience takes the strategy of conversion to a whole new level. What I am still going through now was once so devastating to me that I searched every place I could to find answers; answers on how to feel better about it; answers on how to put it back together, in my terms.

Regarding my current difficult circumstance, I found myself in an extremely serious situation, from my perspective. I wanted advice, despite knowing that the greatest value would be in overcoming it on my own. And still there were times I would have sold my realization, my growth, for an instant fix, for a magical, immediate solution to this problem. Yet, only two weeks later, I stopped thinking that way. I do not want an instant fix or magical solution. I honestly didn't think about how much the situation would make me grow, beyond "fixing" it, until I started talking to you. The revelations that have already come from my search for answers to this situation are indescribable. They cannot be bought for any amount of money, and I know this.

So many people are hurting, and they don't have to. I have read that, on average, one person takes his or her life every 40 seconds. This means that almost 800 thousand people are dying every year, and not one has to. Real lives and real dreams are being ended prematurely because people can't see who they really are from where they stand. I believe I now have the ability to change all of this, thanks to you, of course. I'm more excited about what I can do for others than I've ever been in my life.

(My Soul) So beautiful, and you forgot to mention that these people are taking their lives immediately after they have been given, in many cases, their most valuable gifts; gifts that would have made all of their dreams come true if they had followed, not only what you have learned, but what you have now done, as well.

(LS) I know it's true that they take their lives after their greatest gifts, but not many see it this way. They are in unbearable pain. They can't take it anymore, and they can't see a way out. I understand this. I understand this completely.

(My Soul) But you now have a way to help these people.

Please let me give you some advice, here. I know you love extremes, but not everyone can relate to them in the way you do. So, please take helping others in baby steps, especially where someone's life is at stake. Give readers something they can believe in from where they are. Once people understand your philosophy, they will no longer be devastated by the things that would have paralyzed them in the past, and at this stage, they will be able to see the truth in what has happened to them, the true potential. But please be sensitive to those who have lost hope and have given up on life. You don't see yourself as being so different from others, but in many ways, you are. Think of how *they* will see what you say, not how *you* would, especially when it comes to saving someone's life.

(LS) Thank you for sharing that with me. I know you're right about that. Thank you. I don't come across this much, but when or if I ever do again, I will certainly be better prepared.

(My Soul) You are as innocent as a newborn child.

(LS) What? Where did that come from?

(My Soul) Let's move on.

(LS) Are you really going to leave me hanging on your "innocence" remark?

(My Soul) I am! Five years from now, come back and read that statement; and then tell me you don't understand it.

(LS) Deal!

(My Soul) The value you have for the world may be *slightly* greater than you currently believe, and you should be equally excited about what it means for you.

(LS) I am; maybe even more than I should be.

(My Soul) There is no "even more" than you should be. This is not selfish. Taking care of yourself is a step in the right direction for you. You are creating value, and you deserve to receive value for what you create.

(LS) I have so much more I want to ask you. What we've done so far is amazing. This is the most incredible thing that has ever happened to me.

HOW CAN IT BE THAT WE ARE ALL ONE?

I WANT TO ask you about love, but before I do, something has been bothering me, and I want to see what you have to say about it.

I know that we are all one and that there is no separation between any of us. I know that when someone dies, a part of each of us dies, as well. But what about people who intentionally kill others—does that mean the rest of us are killing others, too? I love to think that I am everyone I love and everyone who loves me, but it doesn't feel good to think that I am also those who hurt or even murder innocent people on purpose. If we are all one, am I not a murderer, too?

(My Soul) First, I want to explain that there is much more to all we have been discussing, and your question is a perfect segue to it.

(LS) Synchronicity?

(My Soul) Yes. Synchronicity. It's working all the time. It's much better to be aware than to try to control or even force things.

As you're walking down the street, kicking a stone, the stone is just as much a part of you as what you would call *your* foot, which kicked it. Do you understand?

(LS) If that's really true, it changes everything. Why do you have the word *your* in italics? Isn't my foot mine?

(My Soul) It is, and it does change everything. Do you doubt that it's true? I have *your* in italics because you see your foot as yours, but not the stone.

(LS) I don't doubt that everything is one. It's just hard to see it that way.

(My Soul) It is not possible to see infinity with limited perception. It would be like taking your Jeep and driving to the moon to have lunch. So, you will always come to the end of physical resources, and as you know from our previous discussions, it is what you do at *that* moment, the *end* moment, that defines who you are.

(LS) Do you mean that when we come to what I used to see as our limit, but we keep going, we reach you?

(My Soul) Beautiful! You're getting this. You reach that part of *you* that has no limits. You can call this many things; it is not only me. You can call this infinite power whatever you feel comfortable calling it: God, the Holy Spirit, your Soul, Infinite Intelligence, Source Energy, Unconsciousness, the Universe, Consciousness…. Whatever resonates with you will resonate with me. Where I live, there are no judgments or jealousies, and when you understand what we understand, you won't have them, either. No matter what you sincerely call your "infinity," you are blessing everyone, because we are all your infinity.

(LS) What do I say to those who won't believe any of this?

(My Soul) You can say, "That's beautiful," or, "We know that's perfect," or, "How was your coffee this morning?"

(LS) They would surely think I was being sarcastic.

(My Soul) Asking them how their coffee was is perfect, because you are really asking them if they have awakened, and they would only understand this if they were.

(LS) Oh, my God—you *are* me!

(My Soul) Why do you feel you have to say anything?

(LS) That's true. I don't have to. Yet, suppose they really want to understand but are having a hard time seeing it all, as I do at times.

(My Soul) You, yourself know that simply saying you want to understand something will not get you to understanding. Every part of you must speak the same message, and until you do, what you want will not be visible to you. When they want the answers badly enough, they will get to the end of their physical resources, keep going, and all the obstacles blocking them will disappear.

More appropriately, they will notice that obstacles were never there.

(LS) Ahh…perfect.

(My Soul) Many will get what they need just by reading this book because you have connected for them. You have taken every part of your life to such extremes that you have made it hard on you, but easy for me. We enjoy you, for there is never a dull moment.

(LS) Is that supposed to be funny?

(My Soul) No, you are the funny one, remember? What your peers call your insanity, we call your light.

(LS) Yes, and they would all say, "The light is on, but no one is home."

(My Soul) Only what matters?

(LS) I know, I know! (The truth.)

Okay, you're taking a pretty long time to answer a simple question.

(My Soul) I can promise that the answer to your question is not very simple to you. There is much about it that needed to be said, and there is still so much more.

Do you really need me to tell you that you are not a killer?

(LS) No, of course I know I'm not a killer, but if we are all one, then are we not also killers?

(My Soul) When you say, "I know I'm not a killer," who is the *I* you are referring to? Have you forgotten who you are?

(LS) I know that *I* am everyone, and everyone is *me*, but I'm not getting this.

(My Soul) Okay, there are parts of *us* that *you* have not yet learned to control. When *someone else,* in your terms, is dying of cancer, you say, "They are dying," and we say, "A part of *you* that you have not learned how to control is killing another part of you." When someone intentionally kills someone, it is the same. A part of you that you do not recognize as you and are not able to control is killing another part of you.

(LS) I don't like this, and I'm not really comfortable with it.

(My Soul) I never intended for you to be comfortable with it. This is why you cling to individuality. Individuality is your ego wanting to be noticed, but it is not the truth. To you, death is a horrible thing, and to us it is your complete liberation. This is where you need to have faith. This is where you need to trust us.

(LS) I do trust you completely. I just want to understand, and I still don't understand it completely.

(My Soul) On the day you understand this, bring your Jeep and meet me for lunch on the moon.

(LS) So, on the day I understand this, I will have no limitations?

(My Soul) Perfect.

While you have been asking how it can be that we are all one, you have been touching the answer with every thought and every idea you have ever had.

(LS) What do you mean?

(My Soul) There is no absolute existence. Everything in the universe exists only in relation to something else. When you have an idea about something that you are observing closely, you are not only forming your idea, but you are forming the object, as well. The object you are forming is a part of you, but you cannot see this with physical senses. This is why, when you see something as true, the universe will agree with you by bringing you physical evidence; and when someone else sees the exact same thing as *not* true, the universe will also agree and bring them physical evidence that matches their perception even though it is so much different than yours.

(LS) So, how we see our lives and what we believe is coming next, is forming what's coming next, too?

(My Soul) Of course. That is something you have always known, so let me give you something you have not always known. When you ask someone whether the majority of people in the world are good people or bad people, if their answer is really true for them, it will exactly match their future experience and the type of people they'll meet. So, for example, if you believe the majority of people are good, you will meet mostly good people, and if you believe the majority of people are bad, you will meet mostly bad people. There are no predictions, only creations.

(LS) Yes, but people's answers will reflect what they already feel, so what good does that do?

(My Soul) And that's exactly the point. You see, you believe they feel that way because that's what they've experienced, and I'm telling you that their experiences are the result of their beliefs, and never the cause. Don't evaluate this based on only one person; see how everyone's experiences accurately mirror their beliefs—and even better, how they mirror what they *know* to be true. All experience is a result, and you have complete control, except that you are still pretending you are not in charge.

(LS) The truth is, I do know that, but for some reason I keep forgetting I do. When asked about this, my answer would not always be how I would act.

(My Soul) Meaning that you know this intellectually, but you have not yet learned it on an emotional level.

(LS) Yes, and as a result, it's very hard for us to see that all experience in our world is a result. Walking through the incantations of the complete opposite is so engaging, so magnetic—and not just in words, but in thoughts and actions, as well.

(My Soul) Yes, and this is exactly why you need to control your own thoughts, feelings, beliefs, and actions. This is exactly why you need to be aware of what you are asking for at every moment you can.

This is the best way for most people to ask and if, when doing so, you feel a release of resistance you know you're in a great place.

Give everything you have while living in the state of knowing that what you are working so hard for *must* happen. This means that every rejection, criticism, and disbelief in you is met with a smile, laughter, or however else you would respond to others who don't know what you already know to be true.

Some masters will tell you that you don't need to give everything you have or even try very hard, and they're right; it's not necessary. However, you have found that when you don't give all you have, eventually you lose the belief that what you want *must* come, which causes it all to fall apart. Therefore, giving your all is like taking out insurance on belief or insurance on knowing.

(LS) Yes, I certainly understand that, but there are certain situations in which not trying at all would actually be better for us, right? This has been my experience in certain situations.

(My Soul) Yes, that's exactly right. If it has to do with being rejected in love, you create the result you choose while walking away and as often after that as you can. However, if you're creating a booming business, then sitting on the couch watching movies and eating potato chips is probably not going to get you where you want, regardless of how good you are at matching the vibration—although matching the vibration authentically would get you off the couch.

(LS) Okay, but if we're teaching people how to open to this communication with their soul on their own, how can we help them know when they should give all they can physically and when they should just allow their creation to form by itself?

(My Soul) Anytime you don't know what to do, or even whether to do something, allow us to tell you. We are always letting you know what you need to know, but are you listening? When you should be doing something, we will nudge you. You have done well with this, but there are still times when you don't listen. There are things you "inherently" (thank you) seem to know and others you don't.

(LS) Touché—and no, thank *you*!

LOVE IS NEVER AN EMOTION OF NEED

(LS) WHAT IS love? Can you please help me explain it so that others and I can understand?

(My Soul) Love is your greatest gift. It has been given to you by God so that you may bless yourself and the world by also giving it away.

(LS) I understand that. I wrote it.

(My Soul) No, we did.

(LS) Even better. Maybe you can explain it in more detail so that people who don't currently feel blessed by love can at least start moving in that direction?

(My Soul) You know firsthand now that *everything* happens *for* you and never against you. You know that this is true regardless of what it is, right?

(LS) I do. That doesn't mean I'm going to like it or that I'm not going to get hurt by it, but I do know that everything occurs for our ultimate realization.

(My Soul) If you want to do more than just learn from an experience, if you want to grow from it, in your terms, you must do more than extract a lesson or think differently about what has happened. You know this in retrospect from your response to being bullied as a kid, and you can look back now and see what your response has done for you and many others. You know this from the experience that made you a writer, as well as your current experience and situation.

(LS) Yes, I know that the greatest gifts have come from listening to feeling and synchronicity and acting on what they were telling me to do, but what about love, where does that fit in?

(My Soul) Even for those who don't understand it, love is meant to get you to act when you feel completely rejected and even when you don't know what to do.

(LS) How can love help us do what is good for everyone?

(My Soul) Great question. That is a question that Love would ask. Love always wants everyone to realize or become *aware* of of who they have always been and display that awareness as real in their life lived.

There is always an appropriate way to love everyone, but instead, too many give up. When someone says, "But he told me he doesn't love me," everyone teaches them that that they must learn to *accept* that, and yet, none of any of this is about love, least of all accepting something you never wanted. It is not possible for love to be rejected. Love has never been about what you get, and when your love is completely about *loving*, without even a thought of what you will receive, you will not be able to stop love from coming to you. But if you keep talking about *us*, sending cute love quotes, and persisting—this is mostly *not* a good idea. There is a time and place for persistence, and you need to clearly know when that is. I know you know this, but I'm mentioning this here for the benefit of those who don't.

(LS) Thank you. Explain how love can never be rejected.

(My Soul) Love is faith and *knowing* at the highest level. Love is not one dimensional. When someone says that their love has been rejected, they are talking about what they believe love to be, but it cannot be love without faith and knowing. Only fear can be rejected, and fear is love's only true opposite.

(LS) I posted this to my page: "You will be loved in direct proportion to the authenticity of your love, along with the depth of the hearts you touch."

It was widely received, but some have taken it personally, thinking that if they are not loved, it is because their love is not real, or it is because they don't touch anyone. What is the truth here? What are we all missing?

(My Soul) The answer is in your question. What is missing is the truth. Most of *your* life, the truth has been missing with you, as well. And in some areas, it still is, but there is a way to change this, and you explain it well in your writing. As you now know, it is not easy to get to the truth.

(LS) Okay, but help me out here. How can we change this?

(My Soul) The most difficult love for all of you is romantic love because you get emotionally attached really fast, so the best place to start is to *choose* to love someone with whom you have no emotional attachment. Make a decision to do something for someone without caring at all what they say, do, or how they react. Do this just to see how it feels.

Ironically, it is the emotional attachment that causes what you call love to *not* be.

What I mean is the emotional attachment to a *need*. It's fine for your heart to explode with love, as long as it continues to do so when you are rejected. Emotion is a huge part of love, while emotional *attachment* is no part of love. Attachment is the *need* to have something a specific way, and that is exactly what fear is.

(LS) It is not easy to learn the distinction between need and choosing, but it is beautiful once you do.

(My Soul) Love is never an emotion of need, but an emotion of faith; or better yet, love is *knowing* at the highest level. You (all of you) have been given the greatest gift that has ever been given to anyone, and you know that you have it, but you can't seem to open it. You know the gift is in your hands, but you believe the gift is worthless to you. You see others who have opened this gift, and they are the happiest people you have ever seen. They think the gift is only for a select few others, and they believe that this gift is just not meant for them.

I have seen you in so much pain because of this in your past, and I have seen you frustrated about it for others' sake once you finally figured it out. People don't know how close they are. They are dying of thirst with their hands all over the water fountain, but they can't find the button that pushes the water out, so they erroneously believe the water is not for them.

(LS) I know. I see this every day with many people, but no matter what I say, most keep doing the same thing. How do I get them to press the button on the water fountain? How do I get them to open their gift and finally find love?

(My Soul) Love is hidden in a place where those who are looking for it will most likely never find it.

(LS) Why make it so difficult? Wouldn't this world be much better if everyone would just love everyone?

(My Soul) Don't you understand that this is just like what you used to call your worst nightmare, your situation that started this entire conversation?

(LS) No, I don't see that at all. How is this like my situation?

(My Soul) Love is not only your greatest gift, but it is also your road map to your mission in life. Your mission in life is to be a forever higher version of your personality. You must puzzle this out on your own. Just as in your "situation," you cannot borrow or buy your way out of it. That would deprive you of your true identity. It would deprive you of your growth, from your perspective, and of your realization from ours. It would also deprive the world of, not only a philosophy, but a heart and mindset they would yearn for if they knew it existed. Giving you what you have not earned is the worst thing we can do "to" you and everyone else. Who would know more about this than you?

You have been on both sides of it, and you know it doesn't work; it hurts everyone.

(LS) That is beautiful! Thank you so much.

Can you explain what you meant by, "It would deprive you of your growth, from your perspective, and of your realization from ours?"

(My Soul) Sure. Not only is every one of your situations always perfect, but contrary to your beliefs, we know that you are all perfect, as well. The notion that humans make mistakes is an illusion. You have not yet evolved in a way where you can see that everything you say and everything you do is perfect. Also, everything everyone else says and does is perfect.

To answer your question: Because you still see yourself as human and therefore imperfect, you think you need to grow, and we know that you are perfect and that all you need to do is remember. (Re-member = put back together) who you are or *realize* who you have always been.

(LS) Okay, but wait a second! I do know that every situation is perfect for us. I have learned that in a really huge way here, but everything I have ever said or done has been perfect, too. How can this be? How can it be that, for instance, when I know I said the wrong thing on an interview and didn't get the job I know I needed, how can this be perfect?

(My Soul) Your physical senses could not perceive how not getting the job was perfect for you. You might say, "But my kids were starving and I needed to feed them," and this is where you need to trust, need to have faith. The understanding that everything leads to a forever higher realization of your personality will not always take away the pain, but once you understand our language and you have the faith and courage to move in that direction, you will always be blessed. You know this. You know that this is not about saying the *wrong* thing on an interview. It is about the *situation* that saying what you call the *wrong* thing in an interview put you in; and you know from experience that all situations are perfect. Is this starting to make sense to you?

(LS) Yes! Thank you.

Let's get back to love. Why is love so misunderstood and so elusive?

(My Soul) Simple. You all want to receive love and the only way to receive love is to give away all the love that is inside you, without the need, or even the desire, for "reciprocation."

(LS) But what about when we love someone so much that all we want is to be loved by that person? Is it really wrong to want to be loved by them?

(My Soul) Wanting to be loved by someone is never wrong when it is a choice. The desire to be loved is not wrong, but when it does not include knowing, it has just not reached the highest level of love, yet. Do you see this?

(LS) I think so. Love is the highest level of *knowing*, and so any *desire* to be loved that does not include knowing, or faith, is not yet love, right?

(My Soul) People love to the degree that they can. When they do love, people love from the part of love that adores, not always the part that includes knowing. Love is not only something that happens to us; it is also something that we must grow into. So, when people say they were rejected by the one they love and are in pain because of it, although they may be in pain, it is not possible for love to have anything to do with it. You get to decide the meaning of what anyone says or does to you. No one can reject you without your permission.

(LS) You make love sound so complicated. Anyway, I'm happy we're talking about this, because when I say this, people take it as meaning that they should just keep talking about *us* and ignore the rejection, as if nothing had been said. And this is the worst thing to do. This is not what I meant by, "no one can reject you without your permission."

(My Soul) Why don't you just explain what you mean?

(LS) The complete explanation is something I don't think too many people would even believe, so honestly, I don't even know where to start with it.

(My Soul) Why are you concerned with what people will believe?

(LS) This is going to be a book, and hopefully a book that delivers a message. It would be really nice if the message were believable.

(My Soul) Do you have any doubt about the authenticity of any of your messages?

(LS) Absolutely not. I believe in them with all my heart and in *you*.

(My Soul) What you think the world would not believe is something you have been doing for about forty years now, and quite successfully, I might add. So, go for it. Do what you have been afraid to do. You have the experiences to back it up. You want to show people how powerful they really are, and yet you are afraid they won't believe who they are, and you know they don't believe it now, so your excuse makes no sense to me.

I'm sorry, but it is *you* who doesn't believe who you are, yet. This is much better coming from you than from me or anyone else, so this one is on you, or should I say, *for* you. I believe in you completely, for I know exactly who you are. Don't worry about who is ready or who is not; just write your truth.

(LS) Phew! Thank you. That was awesome. I wish I could be like you most of the time.

(My Soul) It's coming. I promise you can't escape it.

(LS) I mean, while I am still "what I call *alive*."

(My Soul) It's all coming for you. You only have to lose fear. You can start by telling the world what to do with every so-called rejection, and maybe you can take your own advice when those who don't believe you cause you to feel rejected?

(LS) You are very good at getting me to see what I never could before.

(My Soul) I am your truth, and so authenticity is natural for me.

(LS) I'm so glad I met you.

(My Soul) It was inevitable, and it is the same for everyone. Now, stop procrastinating and tell the world what to do when they experience "what they used to call *rejection*." You need to tell this to the world as much as you need to hear it. Eventually, you will understand that telling it to the world *is* you hearing it.

(LS) Okay, here goes.

When I was much younger and I was rejected, I was not persistent. I would just walk away, devastated, and the walking away part was right, but the devastation was something I eventually learned did not serve me. There are exceptions, but for the most part, anyone who continues to talk about *us* after being rejected is making things worse. Now, I'm not talking about couples who are married or in a committed relationship. Mostly, I'm talking about people who have not been together as a couple, although parts of this philosophy apply to everyone. Every relationship is different, so there is not one rule to follow for all of them.

Eventually, I came to understand that I was rejected and hurt, *not* because I loved the person, but because I *didn't*—at least not completely. Love is a gift from God that comes with an indescribable peace, and only those who have experienced it know what I'm talking about. The part of love that we don't yet understand is an achievement; it is something we must learn to grow into. Our evolution will eventually get us there, but diving into this subject and studying love will get you to understand what most people currently do not understand. You will begin to understand the side of love that is the highest level of faith, or even better, the highest level of *knowing*.

Unquestioned *knowing* is a level of love that brings with it the only ingredient that makes what we have always called love, real. Unquestioned knowing is not ignoring the truth, but instead, it is knowing the complete truth. Being in a place where you can see the complete truth about yourself and what you are capable of, without the voices of your loved ones still ringing in your ears about how you need to be more *realistic*.

Ironically, the further away you are from what your friends and family call being realistic, the closer to realistic you will actually be.

Love is not the opposite of hate. Fear is love's only true opposite. So, armed with this understanding, what do we do when we are faced with what we once called a rejection? Let me give you an example of what I did in this exact situation.

I fell in love with someone who told me that she would never love me. "You are not someone I could ever love," she said to me. This time, I did something different. I did nothing to try to change her mind, or heart, as the case may be; instead, I completely disappeared. I walked away, not in devastation, but rather because I decided to use what I have learned. I decided to create what I wanted in complete silence. We are always closest to our soul and God in complete silence. We are one with God's universe, infinite intelligence, and energy source. I did not call, write her emails, or text. I made certain that we didn't "accidentally" bump into each other in person, as well.

I completely withdrew all physical forms of contact and proceeded to create a different form of contact, one that no one other than I could reject. I silenced the outside world and used what I had learned to create what I wanted, and I did it every day. I did not feel compelled to contact her in any way, even to see if what I had been doing was working. Doing so would have been an action of a lack of faith and I would have risked un-creating all I had been working on. I simply created the result I wanted daily and lived my life by that. One day, unexpectedly, I received a phone call from her, telling me that she loved me.

Now, to be completely honest, it wasn't exactly what I wanted. By the time I received the phone call, what I originally wanted had changed. I was very happy with the result, and in the end, I wanted no more from her than I had received.

You can teach this to anyone who is ready, but it does take a truckload of self-discipline to follow through.

(My Soul) That was beautiful. Why were you so reluctant to write it?

(LS) Well, it's not only *my* business. I don't feel comfortable talking about the details, and there are many details I don't remember. It was a long time ago, and it took more than a year for me to receive that phone call.

(My Soul) I'm quite sure you will tell what you feel to be appropriate to tell. Why do you feel the need to talk about what is so private to you? Do you have any doubt about what happened?

(LS) Absolutely not. I've done this many times. Can you imagine how belittling it would be for the person who made that phone call to even *think* I am saying that her call was not sincere, but had been manufactured by me?

(My Soul) Is that the way it works?

(LS) No! Not at all. The call was both sincere and created by both of us. The result was a co-creation.

(My Soul) Ahh…beautiful.

THE PURPOSE OF LOVE

(LS) CAN YOU explain to me and anyone who might read this what the purpose of love is?

(My Soul) The purpose of love is the same as the purpose of everything. Everything in your life is there to help you realize who you have always been. Realizing it means becoming aware of it and displaying it as real. Love is the ultimate path to purpose. Love will cause you to do things that you would never even attempt to do without it, and action is what completes your faith; action validates and confirms your faith.

Love is the ignition that sets your world on fire. Love is meant to be your ignition, but a lot depends on your faith, or unquestioned knowing. What will you do when your love is tested? When you believe love has caused you pain, will you fold, or will you rise to the level of what love really is? I wait patiently to see if you are ready for love, or if instead you need more experiences. I rejoice even while you don't choose love, knowing that it is inevitable that you will in time.

You choose love by listening to what *we* (myself, your heart, and God) are saying through feeling and synchronicity and having the courage to move in that direction; even if ever so timidly, even if not yet a complete commitment. A complete commitment ultimately will have to come, but a start in the direction of *converting* a rejection, in your terms, and *embracing* it, in ours, is all that is initially needed.

(LS) Yes, I really get this, but what do you mean by *converting* in my terms and *embracing* in yours?

(My Soul) This is something you have just learned, but maybe you have not fully absorbed it yet, so I will go over it again.

(LS) Yes, please.

(My Soul) You still see certain situations as negatives that need to be converted to positives, and we see them as gifts to be embraced.

(LS) Ahh…yes, I do get that. Thank you for reminding me. As Neale Donald Walsch says in *Conversations with God:* "God sends nothing but angels," right?

(My Soul) If you are looking to give him credit for what was in his book, yes, you are right; but if you want the truth, the three of *Us* said it.

(LS) The three of *Us?*

(My Soul) The Father, the Son, and the Holy Spirit, and this includes more than three, do you understand this?

(LS) Yes, I think I do. We are all one.

(My Soul) Absolutely; and you will experience this to the degree that you believe you are.

(LS) Is this why so many people think I'm crazy?

(My Soul) Take your pick. The menu is long, but you're in good company.

(LS) Are you saying that you would have the same problem if you were in my world?

(My Soul) Absolutely not, but I would have the same *experience.*

(LS) Thank you.

(My Soul) Do you see how you create *problems* where none ever existed?

(LS) I do now, thank you.

Okay, getting back to what we were talking about: isn't it true that we can, as you say, *convert* or *embrace* without knowing we are, and without understanding your language of feeling and synchronicity?

(My Soul) You may not consciously know that you have learned our language, but if you're taking the appropriate actions in the direction that serves you and us in terms of your path to our mission for you, then you have understood our messages to you.

(LS) Don't we need to understand the process?

(My Soul) There is no need, but it would certainly help you to understand. Understanding will ensure that you are never lost. Knowing the process gives you a way to get back there whenever you *feel* you need or want to.

Yesterday, you went to Angelo's in Ridge Hill, and you were amazed at how your daughter's boyfriend was handling his gift, and although he *may* not see it as his gift, he is still converting a bad situation into a huge blessing. He is not just doing this for him; do you see how the entire world benefits even from his *attempt?* We don't see this as converting a bad situation into a good one, as most of you would; we see him *embracing* his gift.

(LS) I was just thinking about this situation, and yes, I do see that. I write about it, remember?

(My Soul) Yes. "Even the *failed pursuit* of any dream affects the universe in a way yet unseen." It's a great quote, but in reality, there can be no failed pursuit, and this is why we put it in italics.

(LS) Touché. And, of course, there are no failed experiences.

"As the flower leans toward the sun, it knows without having to ask anyone's advice that it is making its contribution to, not only other flowers, but the expansion of the entire universe." — Love Story and his Soul.

(My Soul) Yes, exactly, only you do not need to sign my name with yours, for once you have been introduced to me, I am implied as you in everything you say and do.

(LS) These sound like such great phrases, and I know they are right just through feeling, but can you explain what it is that makes them right so I can understand more and everyone else can get it, too?

(My Soul) Absolutely. Do you remember what your former predicament has done for you, or do you have to go back and read the pages where we spoke about it again?

(LS) No, of course, I remember.

(My Soul) Think of your situation relative to the question you just asked me about. You have not even come close to what you have set out to accomplish, and look what the pursuit of your goal has already done for you. You had to become more from where *you* stand and *remember* who you always have been from where *we* stand, and you have done this. You may not have come close to accomplishing *your* goal, and yet you are accomplishing ours every day. In the pursuit of what you want for you, you are realizing more of what we want for you every step of the way. Do you see how this works?

(LS) Yes, I do, but I still don't see how everyone else benefits from what has already been done. I can see the potential of everyone benefiting, depending on what I do from here, but how does everyone benefit from what has already been done, now?

(My Soul) We have already spoken about this. What you see of your world is an illusion. Your perception of the world is limited by your physical senses. You see that there is a separation between you and *other people* and between you and *other things,* but what you perceive is not reality. When you hurt yourself, you hurt everyone else; and when you grow or, more accurately, when you *realize,* you cannot do so without everyone else coming along.

(LS) I do see this now, and I have for some time, but it took me a while to get to this point. How will everyone else get here? Can you give me a concrete example so that, instead of me just feeling it, I can have a new dimension as a frame of reference—and so everyone else can, too?

(My Soul) I can, but eventually I'll get to a place where you can no longer relate, and I may already be there now, not only for your readers, but for you, as well.

(LS) Then, take us to our limit here, and I will scream "Uncle!" when I think we've had enough.

(My Soul) The relationship between you and me is a relationship between not only everyone, but also everything. Everything in your world is alive, moving and a world unto itself. Some of this you can see with your physical eyes, and some you cannot. In a perfectly coordinated collaboration, you create your soul as your soul creates you. Just as musicians create music while the music creates them, one does not follow the other; they are always simultaneous creations. All musicians intuitively know this, whether they are aware that they know it or not. This, by the way, is true for everyone, not just musicians. As a writer, you are becoming increasingly aware that this is true.

(LS) This is amazing. Let me see if I understand this. One person's growth, creation, or realization is everyone's, right? If this is so, how does the rest of that person (all of us) become aware of that realization or gain the ability to tap into it?

(My Soul) Exactly, and such a beautifully worded question! The creator is creating me, and I am part of you and everyone and everything, so you would simply connect to me, as you have done, to gain access to this great reservoir of knowledge, talent, and intellect.

(LS) We can have access to the talents of others? How can this be?

(My Soul) You are a part of them that they don't consciously relate to, so from the moment they acquire a talent, the talent is instantly in you, and your access to that talent is loving what they do while connecting to me.

(LS) Uncle!

(My Soul) You're getting it; I know you are. Did you forget that you could not have a thought or feeling that I am unaware of?

(LS) I am getting it, and I *love* it, but I'm afraid we might be losing people here. I don't want this book to get lost in the Martian section of the bookstore.

(My Soul) Well, this book is written by someone from your planet and someone from beyond all the other planets, so you may have to create a section of the bookstore that has not yet been created if you're looking to be accurate.

(LS) New Age replaced by New World, maybe?

(My Soul) Let's get back to the subject at hand. Why did you scream "Uncle!" when what I said was clearly resonating with you?

(LS) I loved what you were saying and it makes a lot of sense to me, now, but I was more concerned with how it would be received by others.

(My Soul) All are on their own journeys at their own pace, and you need to remember that what they believe at every moment is perfect for them. Just like you, they cannot skip lessons. Everyone's beliefs serve them in the moments that they have them.

You are on an adventure to authenticity and you are still looking to see who is more right. Authenticity is right! Everyone's authentic beliefs and authentic desires are right. The one whom you would still refer to as my superior has impeccable timing.

(LS) How can you so accurately describe what I think and what you know? No—don't answer that; it was rhetorical. My God, I had forgotten about that. I do know it, but I don't know why I keep forgetting it.

(My Soul) You forget it when you are caught up in the need to be right.

(LS) I really thought I was completely done with that.

(My Soul) You're getting closer every day. My words to you are not a spanking, merely the truth.

(LS) Thank you very much. As much as it sometimes hurts, I do want the truth.

(My Soul) I know you do, and I promise you that a time comes when the truth no longer hurts. You are closer than you think.

(LS) I feel that I am, because all of the truth is beautiful to me, even when it hurts.

(My Soul) Also, the more you put your heart and *me* into whatever you are striving for, the faster everyone becomes more along with you, that is, the faster everyone comes to realization. And this, of course, works the same way from others to you. Does this make sense to you?

(LS) Yes, that part I knew, but before we get too far away from this, you know there are people who will not let go of the illusion that everything is either right or wrong.

(My Soul) Yes, and you need to understand that this is right for them during the time they believe it.

(LS) Yes, I understand that it serves them to believe it at that time.

(My Soul) Exactly. Contrary to what some believe, they are not wrong. They are right for them. Eventually all of you will see that right and wrong have been replaced by "does this empower me or disempower me."

(LS) So, empower and disempower are the new right and wrong?

(My Soul) Empowerment is always what serves you, and the *need* to be right *never* does. I know not everyone sees it this way, and that's okay. Everyone sees what is right for them in the moment.

Let's get back to where we were. I was saying that, even without making a visible impact, you are still having a huge impact.

If you want to help everyone progress, as well as play your role in the expansion of the universe, just work on you. Become more; become a better version of you. Create a self-improvement boot camp for you. While doing this, always keep in mind—or more appropriately—*in heart*, that whether or not you get where you say you want to go, your impact on the universe and everyone and everything in it is immeasurable, regardless of the results you see.

Don't you understand that there is no failure? Every attempt at something is a success, for it moves what you call *everyone* (and what we call *all one*, closer to realization.

(LS) Is this why we have love?

(My Soul) Now you are getting it. Love guarantees the expansion of the universe. You were all born with built-in desires, and yet many of you still allow society to choose for you.

(LS) And so, it is your job to get us back?

(My Soul) Absolutely. No matter what it takes. Nothing is more important than your mission, and your path to your mission expands everything.

(LS) This is beautiful. I still can't believe it is happening. I know you say I am you, but I was never able to arrive at these answers until we started speaking.

(My Soul) Our communication is not something new. Only your awareness of our communication is new.

(LS) Yes, and the awareness gives me direction, meaning, and purpose. When I thought I was talking solely to myself, I didn't think of my answers as valid.

(My Soul) You were and are talking solely to yourself, and your answers are still more valid than you have ever been aware. This is what your adventure to authenticity is all about: awareness of the truth and then the courage to live from that truth.

(LS) Yes, that is what I want. That is what I want to do.

WHY LOVE EXISTS

CAN YOU PLEASE explain to me what happened over the last four months leading up to January 4, 2016, when friends who I thought were good friends were gone in an instant, as well as the closest relationship I have had in a very long time? It's hard for me to wrap my mind around everything that happened and why it happened. That relationship and that love were so beautiful in some ways that they cannot be described without experiencing them. We made love in all kinds of ways, and I'm talking about ways that do not include sex: the real intimacy.

We did this experiment where we looked into each other's eyes without touching or looking away for three minutes, and in exactly that time, my face was drenched with *her* tears exploding out at me. Words have no shot at describing what that felt like. Not even in movies have I seen anything come close to it. We would laugh for hours in each other's arms and hold each other up when our knees got weak from laughing too much. When we could not physically be in the same place, we would laugh for hours on the phone until we were so exhausted we could not keep our eyes open. It appeared that the energy from her heart was constantly flowing through to her personality, which lit up every room she walked into. And there was much more.

It all started unraveling so quickly. She needed me to give her something I couldn't give her, and although I never understood why, I didn't judge her. We cried in each other's arms for about three days, knowing that three days was all we had left with each other. Although it was painful and exhausting, I thought it was quite beautiful: two people with no anger anywhere, until, of course, that changed, and then loving each other enough to help the other through the pain. I had just as many of her tears on my face as she had my tears on hers.

I have many questions about this. Why couldn't this beautiful love last a lifetime? Do you have any idea how amazing that would be? Why couldn't she just let me be me?

(My Soul) Obviously, you do not have any idea how amazing exactly what happened was. She was supposed to do what she did. Everyone was supposed to do what they did. It is not possible for something better to have happened.

(LS) I do try to see everything that happens as perfect, but it's not always easy.

(My Soul) Understand that when it's not easy for you, it's because you are seeing what happened through the eyes of *your* mission instead of the eyes of *our* mission.

(LS) What do you mean by that?

(My Soul) Whenever you have difficulty finding the meaning in any situation, it is only because you want to change what is real instead of understanding it. Eventually, you will get to a place where you love all that is real, love all that has "already" happened, love the present moment.

Your present is a gift that cannot be returned; love each of them completely. Only when you love every present you have been given will every moment of your life make you smile.

(LS) I know I'm not there yet, but I'm much closer than I was a year ago, and it feels really good to be where I am, now. It's not that I don't get hurt, as you would certainly know, but at least I can understand your message to me now, although I do have other questions.

We were dating for about three months and we were in New York having a great time, but it was over. We had opposing beliefs on a certain subject, and neither of us was willing or able to accept the other's view. This was not about which of us was right; it was simply that her view was not acceptable to me and mine was not acceptable to her. We were both devastated, and in her state of devastation, she went to lunch with two of my friends, and they never were the same toward me again. I had loved going to their restaurant, but now, the entire dynamic has changed, and it no longer felt right to be there.

I would love to know why my friends turned on me so quickly? Why did they not call me and talk to me? Why didn't they ask me how I felt? I thought they knew me well, and yet they just accepted as gospel what someone else had said, someone they had just met.

(My Soul) It doesn't matter what was said or done. I promise you, no one has turned on you. When you see the complete perfection in all that happens, you will forever know that everyone loves you.

(LS) I can easily tell you at least two people who hate me, and possibly more, now.

(My Soul) And regardless of what they say or do to support that, you would *all* be wrong. What you call your "former" friends are more your friends now than they were before. Don't you understand that someone had to play that role so that you could have this experience? They knew you needed this to grow, and so they accepted this role for you.

(LS) I'm guessing that where and when these decisions are made, no one ever worries about how others will see them.

(My Soul) Exactly! All of you only worry about how you are seen where you live, never where I live.

(LS) I know we're not finished with this subject, but eventually I would love to know if I can completely live where you live without having to experience what we call dying, first?

(My Soul) Of course, you can, and that is the largest part of your adventure to authenticity. Eventually you all will know that love is the only authentic experience. You have heard Brian Weiss say, "Only love is real." Also, there is no dying. What you call dying is what we call your awakening.

(LS) That is beautiful. I know. We wrote about this: "Dying is not when we sleep forever, but when we are forced to wake up to what we never understood when we thought we were awake."

(My Soul) So perfect! Yes, that is unmistakably us.

(LS) Wait—let's get back to my new situation.

(My Soul) Please! I live for your "situations." If it wasn't for you, I would probably be bored out of my mind.

(LS) Ha-ha-ha! Oh, my God, you are funny. I aim to please.

(My Soul) Needless to say, your aim is quite good. You can be the dart-throwing champion of your planet if you choose.

(LS) Okay, the Love Story roast is a little well done, by now. The comedic aperitif is now over. Time to get back to chomping on the main course.

(My Soul) As you wish.

UNCONDITIONAL LOVE

(MS) WHAT DO you want to know about next?

(LS) I can't see how this knowledge benefits my friends. Can you help me understand it better?

(My Soul) What about you? Don't you think we should start with you, first?

(LS) Yes, please start wherever you want.

(My Soul) Do you see how your body reacts when you read the words, "Don't worry, I won't expose you?"

(LS) Yes, initially, but I caught myself.

(My Soul) Yes, you did catch yourself; but my point is that your initial reaction was to become the presupposition that you were presented with (exposed). Did you notice that? This is something that we know is extremely important for you. You may not completely understand why, yet, but I promise that you will. There are times you get entranced by the unquestioned congruency of presuppositions.

(LS) It might help if you used words I can actually understand. If I keep having to switch to the online dictionary, my readers will be dead before this book gets published.

(My Soul) Honestly, you should be putting a lot more than eight hours a day into this.

(LS) Ugh. Okay, slave driver, let's get back to this.

(My Soul) I neither need nor ask you for anything. You keep talking about being under pressure, but your actions speak of not much more than a stroll in the park.

(LS) A little exaggeration, but point taken.

(My Soul) Okay, you know what the words mean, and I know you agree with "becoming the presupposition." Once you caught your initial reaction, you were fine, and it didn't take you too long this time.

(LS) My initial reaction felt as if I had been sent pictures of clouds in the sky along with the message, "Look what you've done to me." I mean, it was like a little boy hands Mother Teresa a piece of paper that says, "Don't worry, I promise I will not expose you." And, of course, Mother Teresa just puts her hand on the boy's shoulder and says, "You're such a beautiful child. I love you."

(My Soul) I am on board with everything you just said, except I think the Mother Teresa thing is a little stretch. You will need a lot more than a sex change operation to be a Mother Teresa.

(LS) You are hilarious! Maybe we can do standup together. I can use the money. But if you get stage fright, I'm going to have to kill you.

(My Soul) I'm already what you would call dead.

(LS) That's a big help.

Anyway, I can't wait until I feel comfortable enough to be completely exposed, so long as what is being exposed is the truth. I am completely comfortable with almost everything, except for one fairly large thing right now, but I'm working toward that every day. That is what this book is about; exposing my truths, the good and what some might still call the bad.

I want my close friends and family to know the truth, but I do not feel sorry for myself, and I don't want anyone else to feel sorry for me. Initially, I thought that telling my friends about my situation would make things awkward; apparently, I was very wrong about that. Apparently, those I have told really do love me unconditionally. I wanted to tell the truth to everyone about where I *was* when I was not there anymore. Does this make any sense?

(My Soul) To you, maybe.

(LS) But not to you?

(My Soul) I understand that from where you are it is easier for you to move forward and take care of all you still say you want to take care of, without having to contend with everyone else knowing, but you are still doing things you don't have to do, and these things are hurting you. Not only are you deceiving others, but you are still deceiving yourself.

When you are truly honest with yourself, you will admit that you are not just saving others from feeling bad, but you're saving yourself, as well. You will come clean to yourself about your level of commitment to accomplishing all you say you want to accomplish.

(LS) I know you're right, and I know I've been having a problem getting there. I want more than anything to fully commit, and I know we've spoken about this before. I have moments of full commitment, but they don't last long enough.

(My Soul) You have *never* fully committed when you continuously start and stop.

(LS) How do I start and never look back?

(My Soul) Many people do the same thing, but most of them stop trying eventually, and we *know* you will never stop trying. You met a man in the airport, yesterday, who told you that he no longer makes any New Year's resolutions because he never keeps them. The point is not to stop making the resolutions, but to learn how to keep them.

(LS) Yes, I know this. Only through persistence can we realize who we are.

(My Soul) Is that so? Can you tell me more about that?

(LS) Touché!

(My Soul) Seriously, tell me about this, but do it without using any words, unless absolutely necessary. Feel your love and level of commitment. It is such a beautiful thing.

(LS) Deal!

(My Soul) It is perfectly okay to do this in your own time. You have all of the knowledge and ability to accomplish *anything* you choose; you just need to fully make that choice without unmaking it.

And, please, refrain from verbalizing how committed you are to the world until the rest of you can speak of the same commitment.

(LS) Perfect, thank you.

(My Soul) So, are you clear on why every part of everything that happened is such a blessing to you?

(LS) I'm not sure about every part, but the closer I look at what initially hurt me so much, the more I see the magnificence in it all.

(My Soul) It is quite beautiful to witness your revelation. You are my masterpiece, while I am your hammer and chisel, and I have been recruited to remove those parts of you that are no longer necessary so that your character traits can be honed, clearly defined, uncovered, and finally visible to you and the world.

(LS) Your "words" are a masterpiece.

(My Soul) So, tell me how you feel now about everything that happened.

(LS) There are times I completely understand it all, and I really do want all of them to be happy, but there are still times when I get angry about it. I believe I know who arranged all this. In fact, I have no doubt about it. It was not one person, but a group of people (souls), and I know not all of them are consciously aware. There are so many things that could not possibly have been a coincidence. I can see so much more than I could when I wrote about it earlier in our conversation, and somehow I suspect that there's even more to come.

(My Soul) I know we spoke about this before, but you just uncovered this at a level where you know, without any question, what the truth is. Do you realize what you've just done? You have discovered a new world, a world in which everyone already lives, but no one knows they do.

(LS) This is incredible! Does everyone really do this? I've only had this experience with one person, and I've never heard of anyone having an experience even similar to it?

(My Soul) Oh, yes, you have had this experience many times, and so has everyone else.

(LS) Really? And it took me this long to notice? Actually, I was talking about one experience that I was aware of, but I didn't know I had others, as well.

(My Soul) The conversation that led you to me was one that you noticed, and you're about to discover another one very soon.

(LS) Oh, my God! I forgot about that. I'm going to discover another one? Who? When?

(My Soul) Be patient. It will make itself known to you very soon. This is pretty valuable, so why don't you tell the story from the beginning so everyone reading this can learn about this amazing new world you discovered.

(LS) Okay, where do I begin? When I was much younger, my uncle tried to teach me many things. I really learned a lot, but I was stubborn about some things, as well. There were many things I never listened to. "You and I are different; your actions on my personality won't match," were my words to him. My uncle died in 1988, and in 2010, I met a woman who became my best friend for almost six years. I was sometimes asked, "Is this a girlfriend, or just a friend?" My answer was always,

"Neither." There was never anything romantic going on, but she was so much more than just a friend; she was family to me. Our friendship was often misunderstood, because no one could believe that two friends would do so much for each other and want nothing in return. This was beyond what many people could comprehend. She understood my journey in a way that no one else did, and she was excited about helping me stay on the path that would ultimately become my adventure to authenticity.

I started to notice that she was trying to teach me many of the same lessons about life as my uncle had many years ago. She even used exactly the same words, at times. Once when I was driving her home, I said, "Are you sure you don't know my uncle?" My uncle had died more than twenty-two years before I asked this question, but her words and advice made it feel as if he were in the car. I looked up and saw my uncle's name on a street sign about two blocks away from her house, and it's not a common name; in fact, it is very uncommon. As crazy as this might sound, the incident never felt spooky to me. It was actually comforting to know that I was being taken care of by people who loved me, and I had a sense of peace that I was safe. I'm pretty sure this took place in 2010.

(My Soul) Your recognition of the purpose of all that has happened in your life has given you a glimpse of how powerful we all are. Do you see this?

(LS) Yes, I do, and I love this.

It's taken me a long time and a lot of pain to get here. I have had experiences in which people help me, while on the outside they appear to be trying to hurt me, but everything they do to hurt me ends up benefiting me in some way. What is this and how does this happen?

(My Soul) When you become aware that this is happening, it is not the "event" that makes the difference, it's the "state" you are in that makes the difference, because everything benefits you, but only when you can access the resources to see and feel this, only when you can achieve a vibration, or level of energy, that will get you to this awareness. I know there are some horrific things that happen to people and I'm not saying that it's good that it happened. What I am saying is, everything was meant for you to grow, become, realize and we want you to love yourself, but you could not even *be* yourself, without all of your experiences.

(LS) I *do* love myself. I just wish I didn't have to go through so much pain to become me.

(My Soul) You never had to.

(LS) *Now,* you tell me this?

(My Soul) I have always been telling you; it's only recently you started to listen.

(LS) Is it always *my* fault?

No, don't answer that. Instead, tell me more about love. How did love become so magical?

(My Soul) Love is the answer to everything. When you love with no conditions, you make *everything* possible. When you love just because you want someone else to be happy or you want them to grow and become more, you are armed and protected by the power of the universe; you are protected by the power of God. You are more powerful than you have ever imagined, and *love* is the only way to turn on that power. You are about to learn more about this through experience in your life.

The term, "unconditional love" is somewhat misleading; it suggests that there is some form of love that is conditional, and this is just not true. Before you can love, you have to be honest with yourself, and you know how difficult that is. Everyone thinks they're honest with themselves, but most haven't seen themselves, yet. The reasons you "love" someone will determine whether it actually is love, authentic love, in your terms. If you can find a reason, it's probably not love. When you can identify a reason, what happens when that reason's no longer there, is what we called love no longer there too? Ask yourself if your love has even a subtle agenda. You know this well. You have taken your love higher, but many will read this and be confused. People will say, "Why should we love without getting anything in return," not knowing that *giving* love completely is *our* greatest gift, not only to others, but to ourselves, as well.

(LS) Yes, this is exactly right. But those who don't understand this feel empty after giving, and they say it didn't work for them; but even the thought, "It didn't work," means that they were expecting something for it, which means it was not love. Some think I am asking them to sacrifice their lives for someone they may not even know well, and yet, it is the exact opposite. To find a way to give love, even to a stranger, never sacrifices your life; it saves it. How can we get the world to understand this?

A good friend asked me, "What would the world be like if everyone treated everyone else as if they would be dying at midnight?" It is an inspiring thought, one that's even hard to imagine, especially with what's going on in our world today.

(My Soul) And yet, this is exactly the attitude that will save all of you. You have not been honest with yourselves. Generosity only becomes a problem when, instead of being an attempt to help, it is an attempt to be seen the way you want to be seen. This may look good to some people on the surface, but you were hurting everyone, including yourselves. Do you see that, now?

(LS) Yes, I completely understand that, now. Oh, my God, how stupid I was!

(My Soul) Not at all. You and all who don't understand that everything is meant to serve you will say how stupid it was, but once you understand, you will know that every event and circumstance could not be more perfect. The people who have disagreed with the way you've lived your life, which includes you for part of it, would not want to recognize that they were part of that plan, and for good reason: They would imagine that it doesn't "become them," or look good, to have anything to do with your life choices, and yet, that is exactly what it does do. It becomes them in that it aids their realization. You and they *are* and *have been* wrong about this. You have learned that truly loving someone is doing what is best for them, even if they feel it is hurting them. Also, if someone is dying at midnight, money will not help; you actually have to love them. Do you understand this?

(LS) Oh, my God, yes. Wow, that was wonderful. Thank you. People are hurting because they don't understand how *not* helping them in the way they say they want is really helping them. I remember when I felt this way and how frustrating it was not to know the truth, although I have subsequently asked for help that I know doesn't serve me. It's not always easy to be strong. This is the love that I had to learn about, and I had to learn about it from both sides, from giving and receiving. It was not easy for me. It's still not easy, but I'm making progress.

(My Soul) If you want to create a miracle, love when no one in the world would believe it's even possible.

(LS) Yes, we wrote that a few years ago.

(My Soul) Right now is your opportunity for a miracle. The question is, what are you going to do, now? Are you going to continue to find a way to choose love?

(LS) I thought I already did choose love.

(My Soul) Yes, but it's an ongoing decision, one that will, forever take you higher and if you're satisfied with that level of love, then you're done; but I know you can never be satisfied with that.

(LS) No, I want to continue on this path; I want to continue this journey with you, please guide me.

(My Soul) Do you remember how you became a writer?

(LS) Yes, of course.

(My Soul) That was your greatest example of loving while no one would believe it was possible, and look what it has done for you and millions of people already. Trust me when I tell you that, if you're really serious about your message, you have not yet imagined the degree of impact you can have on this world. This, of course, is your choice. You created an action plan to love a woman only for herself, and look what happened as a result of that.

(LS) Yes, I remember that well, but the people on my page didn't understand completely. They all thought I wanted to get her back. It was very obvious that I loved her, but I did not want to get back together with her. I knew if I did, I'd be gone in less than three days. This is where I learned that love is always right, but not necessarily the relationship.

(My Soul) Your initial reaction was not one of love, but you redeemed yourself, and now you have the same opportunity here, if you choose to do anything about it.

(LS) Incredible! I am glad I found you.

(My Soul) You have just experienced what it means to find yourself.

(LS) Touché.

(My Soul) I have noticed the rise in your level of commitment, and this is great. The energy you are now putting into your dreams is perfect. Now, just add more discipline, and you'll be there.

(LS) Ahh. Thank you. I feel much better, and I know what I need to do next. I just have to get myself to do it.

(My Soul) It will come. You will put this together.

(LS) It feels good having you believe in me.

(My Soul) It is nothing more than you believing in yourself.

(LS) I never even thought of that!

LOVING UNCONDITIONALLY
MAKES EVERYTHING POSSIBLE

OKAY, YOU SAID that if we love with no conditions, everything is possible, but how exactly does it happen?

(My Soul) When you love this completely and purely, every cell in your body is affected. Your heart and mind are in every one of your cells, and so you have an army of 50 trillion crusaders, reaching out to the universe and creating from your desires. When your mind and your purest form of love collaborate and occupy every cell in your body, you can make anything happen, and many times you do, all without consciously knowing it.

(LS) Are you serious? Is this really the way it works?

(My Soul) Absolutely! And did you notice that you just became weightless from reading that?

(LS) My God! Yes!

(My Soul) That feeling is your indicator; it tells you that you are in a place that serves not only *you*, but everyone and everything else, as well. That feeling lets you know that you are "on purpose," and of course, both definitions apply, you are on track to your purpose and doing it intentionally).

(LS) Meaning intent and on course?

(My Soul) Yes, intentionally headed toward your mission.

(LS) Cool.

(My Soul) Getting back to the weightlessness you just experienced, this state is fertile ground, or maybe I should say, "fertile air" in your case.

(LS) What do you mean?

(My Soul) When you are on purpose and weightless, whatever you are focusing on is being born; when you are fearful, the same thing is happening.

(LS) Does this mean that we are creating all the time without knowing that we are responsible for our creations?

(My Soul) Please read your question over again as if someone were asking you that question?

(LS) My God, am I in a trance? Yes, I know we all are, but I mean, I should know that we're creating all the time.

(My Soul) I know you've always known that, but you are seeing it from a different perspective, now, and this is rounding you out. Do you see how this is working, how this serves you?

(LS) Yes! Thank you. I knew something was different. Okay, I see that, now.

(My Soul) Because you, specifically, have always had a problem with the way you are seen by those you care about and respect, and even strangers, for that matter. Most often, you have *become* the presuppositions that others have attributed to you. How many times have you lost your identity to the opinions of others? There is no doubt that you have gotten better, but in certain situations where someone doesn't believe in you, you drop who you really are and become the identity the person has chosen for you, instead; at least temporarily. What you're going through is an opportunity to know who you are in the face of what you believe others might think of you—and, of course, so much more. You've always had a problem with this, but you're not the same person anymore. This is a huge challenge for you, and you're ready for it now.

(LS) But asking others for the truth does not guarantee I am being told the truth.

(My Soul) Of course not, but it's better than assuming something without even trying to get the answer. Regardless, this is an opportunity to realize who you are. This is your opportunity to know the truth about you, no matter what anyone says or does, and display it. Do you know what I mean by that?

(LS) Yes, you mean living the truth, not just knowing it.

(My Soul) Exactly! Living your truth means you don't *need* the answer.

(LS) Beautiful, thank you. The only reason I will make that phone call is because I may be assuming something that's not true, just as I believe they have done with me, but I don't know for sure.

(My Soul) There is much more to this than you are admitting to yourself at the moment.

(LS) I am not proud of everything I've done in my life, but I don't regret any of it because I know how the present moment serves me, although I would not want to repeat the choices I am not proud of.

Also, I still have a problem with things that are not true that some have said and others believed. My initial response is still to defend myself, and I don't want it to be this way. I inherently know it should not be this way.

(My Soul) I know you don't want it to be this way, and you're moving in the right direction. Be patient with yourself, but acknowledge that it is not only what is *not* true that you have a problem with.

(LS) Yes, I agree. I am getting better, but at times, the truth still hurts. I honestly don't want to be patient with this. It's way too important for me to put off.

(My Soul) Then, don't put it off. You know exactly what to do, now.

(LS) Earlier in this conversation, I might have asked what is wrong with wanting to be seen for who I truly am, and now I understand that there is nothing wrong with it as long as I don't *need* to be.

(My Soul) Perfect.

(LS) But I still seem to have a problem with this in another arena.

(My Soul) I know, but please explain for everyone.

(LS) Many people have pretended that they know me better than they do and have even gone as far as to pretend that they have been intimate with me. That has always bothered me when, truthfully, it should bother them more. I have always known women to guard their reputations whether what was being said was true or not. To see them lie about themselves, ignoring the possibility that it might hurt them, just to make people believe they were closer to me than they were, is a very ugly thing to me. They're selling themselves out. They are bartering with their character, whatever is left of it, in exchange for being seen the way they want to be seen, and what they don't know is that the way they want to be seen is a lie. I'm not who they think I am. The fantasy is so much better than the reality.

There is a scene in the movie *Notting Hill*, in which Julia Roberts says, "You know, that fame thing is not real." I have a small social media following, and I'm certainly not famous, but in my little world, I completely understand that fame is not real. It took me a really long time to become aware of the effect that *Love Story* has on some people, and it's not at all what I expected—or even wanted.

(My Soul) Do you realize what you described about people lying to themselves and bartering their souls was you in a different arena, just over a year ago?

(LS) I can't believe you just said that.

(My Soul) You have gotten so much further along on your journey that you don't even recognize yourself, anymore.

(LS) I didn't make the connection right away, but you're right. Now I get to see how ugly *I* was. To be fair to me, I didn't lie about anyone, so no one's reputation was on the line.

(My Soul) Are you saying that your choices were a more enlightened form of deception?

(LS) Come on, that is spectacularly unfair.

(My Soul) You lied to yourself and others about who you are, not only in words, but in actions, as well. You have used money to be seen a certain way, and that was a lie just as theirs was. This has been going on for your entire life. Only since you have been aware that you have been on an adventure to authenticity has it come to an almost complete stop.

(LS) As I read your last statement, I can't help thinking that maybe I should get Sarah Palin to endorse my candidacy for president. Please don't take this personally; it's just that your overwhelming admiration for me brings tears to my eyes.

(My Soul) I'm sorry, but the only way you can *run* for anything is if you get a discount card at Foot Locker.

(LS) Come on. Seriously, am I really that bad?

(My Soul) I never said you were bad. You all have your own journeys, and not one of you knows who you are yet, at least not completely.

If you're worried about people degrading you or criticizing you, the only ones who will ever do that are those who are not yet aware of their own truth and, worse, still afraid to face it.

(LS) Oh, my God. That is incredible! Thank you so much.

(My Soul) It wasn't long ago in this conversation that you were asking how your greatest tragedy and worst failure were good for you, and you are telling us many ways throughout this conversation. You are learning how to deal with the unknown.

(LS) That's right, but I am going to do something about it.

(My Soul) You have always said that you believe your aunt and uncle played a role in your associations with your friends. Is this not true?

(LS) Yes, lots of serendipitous things have occurred with many of my friends, and all seem to have a strong connection to my aunt and uncle.

(My Soul) As clearly as you can remember, what would your uncle say to you if he were what you call alive, right now?

(LS) Hm. Yes. "You cannot be responsible for what anyone says or thinks about you. You can only be responsible for the truth." I know this, but I am trying to accomplish something here, and this can hurt my chances at accomplishing it.

(My Soul) You know this, but obviously, you need me to remind you again. When you agree that someone, or something can hurt you, you instantly become co-creators, or in this case, co-destroyers. You and the person, or thing, collaborate, or work together to destroy you. There are no right or wrong decisions; there are only those that empower you and those that disempower you. The "decision" to give anyone the power to hurt you is a disempowering decision, and when you *know* this, it is like *deciding* to be hurt. Does this make sense; maybe even ring a bell?

(LS) Thank you for getting me back.

(My Soul) When the thoughts, words, feelings, and actions of a person reflect those of someone who is not sure, in our language, that is a choice, because you have other options that you are denying you have at the moment.

You have other options that you have forgotten you have.

(LS) What if we don't know we have other options? And even if we did know that, what if we don't know how to choose what we want?

(My Soul) We will get to that when we talk about prayer and affirmations.

READING AND RESPONDING TO
YOUR LANGUAGE OF FEELING
AND SYNCHRONICITY

(LS) LET'S GET to your language and how we should…I mean, how it *will*, benefit us to respond in action.

(My Soul) Ah. Good to see you getting this. You definitely understand the energy to become super-successful. In other words, you make this connection. You understand our language as it relates to you, and you are now also acting on our messages at a high level.

(LS) I do, but let's dig deeper into this. Somehow, I responded to you in the way you wanted me to respond, even many years ago when I had no idea that there was a message. I know that many others do, too, but to become conscious of the message and how we answer back in action is beautiful and would help many people. I remember being lost many times in my life because I was in pain, and I didn't know what to do. Understanding this dynamic will help everyone.

(My Soul) Understanding this dynamic has huge value. It will give everyone something to feel better about while enhancing the energy to reach their dreams, in your world's terms. Hope, even before it gets to faith and ultimately to knowing, can add to this energy as well, but please remember that hope only serves you when you get there from depression or someplace lower than hope, like anger, or frustration. Also, when someone applies this dynamic as a result of reading these words, both you and they become co-creators in the expansion of the entire universe. Do you see this?

(LS) Okay, for example, I am benefiting right now from someone's pursuit of a dream, even when I don't know them and they don't know me and I have no idea where they are or what they're doing.

(My Soul) Very good, except that you do know each other but, are just not aware that you do. Also, I want to be clear about this: even when people think they have completely failed, the energy from their pursuit alone advances not only themselves, but all of humanity, along with everything in the universe, from a grain of sand to the stars in the sky. Absolutely nothing is unaffected by the pursuit of any dream.

(LS) This is unbelievable. It is extremely difficult for any of us to see. What if no one believes any of it?

(My Soul) It is not my responsibility to judge who is ready to accept this and who is not. It is my responsibility to deliver the truth, and I have been doing it for all of you since the beginning of what you call time.

(LS) Let me see if I have this right. If the mere pursuit of any dream advances everything, and if all dreams reside in our hearts, then our hearts are part of the plan for all of progress, all of growth, or realization.

(My Soul) Now you're connecting the dots. Very good. In very much the same way that making love, or even sex, ensures your existence, all the desires that live in your heart ensure the continued expansion of the entire universe.

(LS) Now I think I understand on a different level what you do. When fear or the well-meaning advice of others takes us away from our hearts, you get us back there. And getting back to our hearts is not only for us, but for *everything*. Is this right?

(My Soul) Beautiful. Do you see what this process of getting to the truth is doing for you?

(LS) Yes, and I am not the only one who is benefiting from this.

(My Soul) Perfect. If this book never gets published and no one ever reads another one of your words, you have already contributed to the realization of everything and everyone.

(LS) I have to say that this does make me feel better about the millions of so-called failures I've experienced in this lifetime.

(My Soul) Slight exaggeration. I promise you there were quite a few less than millions of what you still call failures.

Okay, let's get back to where we were. I don't want to get too far off the subject, but there are always many things within each subject that I know I will need to understand.

(My Soul) That's okay. We were talking about releasing resistance.

Know that once anything has been created, it is already real, and your task is complete. This is literally all you need to know about creation.

Just as with unconditional love, love is the art of creating. When you love because you love loving, it is impossible to keep love from coming to you. And when you create for the pleasure of creating, you cannot stop its physical equivalent from appearing.

(LS) There have been times when I was trying to communicate what it means to give up the need for specific results when some people thought I was asking them to give up on their dream. Of course, this is not true, but I can understand why they don't see it this way.

(My Soul) All they need to do to get what they want so badly is to move themselves out of the way. By the way, you do this, too. I have heard you say that you are good at getting yourself out of the way, and you are, some of the time. You will be good at it more of the time when you stop forgetting who you are.

Stop trying to control circumstances, because every time you do, you are telling us not to help you. Every time you start worrying about what might happen, you disconnect one prayer or affirmation and start a new one.

Therefore, when you explain about giving up the need for specific results, just say that you are only helping them to get out of *my* way, out of their soul's way.

Magically, the moment you release the *need* for a specific result, you can literally feel the universe bringing it to you.

Those of you who feel this *release* know what I'm talking about. It is *not* giving up on your dreams; instead, it is the only sure way to realize them. When you learn to give up the emotional *need* of any specific result, whatever you want *must* come. This is *not* giving up on having it, as many might think, it is giving up on *blocking* it. Life is so much easier than you ever thought.

"Allow Me," becomes your action and your answer. When you achieve this state of allowing, you feel weightless, and when you stop trying to control, that is the only time you can be in control.

(LS) That was an impressive explanation. I always feel much better after talking to you. I feel that *release* right now, and I want it to last. What am I doing wrong, and how do I keep that feeling from never leaving me?

(My Soul) Read the appropriate parts of this conversation every day. Or read any parts you prefer. This won't take long, only a few minutes a day, and you'll be fine.

(LS) Isn't it pathetic that I need to read my own book in order to grow?

(My Soul) On the contrary, it's a screaming endorsement.

(LS) So, we really don't have anything to worry about?

(My Soul) I look forward to the day you know how comical that sounds to us.

(LS) It's not funny to any of us.

(My Soul) Not yet, unfortunately. It's like you mowed seven acres of land and missed one blade of grass, and you're worried about being fired. I don't care how badly you think you need the money, being fired should be your loudest celebration.

(LS) How can you say that? Losing income in a family can be a serious thing.

(My Soul) Only when you've forgotten who you are. A real celebration allows us to feel along with you how much you know who you are. It's a display of faith, and it shows how much you trust us.

(LS) You just reminded me of something I wrote almost a year ago that seems to be relevant here.

THE DIRECTIONS TO THE NEXT AMAZING PLACE ON "YOUR" JOURNEY

Put down your map, disconnect your GPS, and turn off your cell phone. The first two, most of us can handle, but turn off someone's cell phone, and they will surely have seizures. We have no distance to travel to get to this amazing place, and yet no one I know is completely there yet, including me, of course. I'm not talking about the cell phone. I have come to understand that the cell phone is the 20th Century, inverse adult pacifier, because it actually makes adults throw temper tantrums and even cry, and yet we are still addicted.

How powerful will you feel on the day you get to the place where the person you hoped would call doesn't and you are still the happiest you have ever been in your life? When you don't get the job or the promotion you are *supposed* to get, buy your favorite champagne or festive treat and celebrate in style. When someone asks you what you're celebrating, you pump your fist, flash you biggest, brightest, sincerest smile, and say—

"I didn't get what I wanted."

We *really* should do this. Don't you understand that we are being tested? Faith is *not* about praying that we will be safe and then going out to buy a bomb shelter. We have all been born to *live*. We have been born to *really live*. I know not everyone can just take off and travel for six months at the moment, *but there is not one person or circumstance in your life now or in your past that has taken control of your emotions.* And if they have, it's because *you* gave it to them. And now, at the first chance you get, you are taking it back.

Let's not live like this anymore, sending an email or text, and when we don't hear back in three minutes, going back and rereading it to see if they possibly could have taken our words the wrong way. This is not living. We are here to *love everyone* and celebrate life. We should instead pray that they take it the wrong way so we don't have to look at our phone anymore. We need to be the gatekeepers of our hearts and minds, knowing that not everyone belongs in our daily lives. If possible, though, we should get to a place where we still love them.

Love *everyone*; because once you grasp this, you know that even those who appear to be trying to hurt you are really helping you. They are getting you to your ultimate destination much more quickly, so long as you do not seek retribution and move backwards. What's going on in your life is what's going on. It has nothing to do with your happiness, and it never did. We were the ones who linked these together.

We have the power. Time to take the power back; it's been in the wrong hands for way too long. Don't you *love* happy people? I certainly do. I am insanely attracted to very happy people. *Please come celebrate "every part" of life with me!* —Love Story

(My Soul) This is great, and it's even better that you remember it now, because you need to get back to living this way.

Too many in your society fear that they are not strong enough, not capable enough, and lack any real power to change their lives. And instead, the only possible fear can be that you are powerful beyond your wildest imagination.

(LS) Thank you so much, and living the truth that we are powerful will be even more amazing.

WHO ARE YOU, MY SOUL, AND WHY DO YOU DO WHAT YOU DO?

(LS) THIS SEEMS like a perfect time to talk about who you are to us and why you do what you do.

(My Soul) Sure.

I am the part of you that has no limits. I am the part of you that lives in a world with no obstacles. Your heart and I are disciples of God, and we speak in the language of feeling and synchronicity while delivering breadcrumbs from heaven.

(LS) Delivering breadcrumbs? Are we having veal parmesan today? Is this what you call "soul" food? You're killing me! Do you realize where I live? There is no Italian food around here, and even if there was, I'm not sure I would have the courage to try it.

(My Soul) I write one word that doesn't look like it belongs here and immediately you go into some kind of comedy routine?

(LS) Please, don't get me started.

(My Soul) I'll watch my step.

(LS) You don't have feet; you should watch where you float instead.

(My Soul) Can we please get back to being serious? It would be a shame to see all this value get lost in the comedy section of a bookstore.

(LS) Of course. Soul forbid a funny guy should be spiritual. (My Soul) Touché.

(LS) With all the *touchés* in this book, they may put it in the fencing section, and I don't mean the white picket variety. I think I might have comedic Tourette's. Okay, okay, just had to get that out of my system. I'm done now.

I've been trying to think of a way to help people understand how to read your language of feeling and synchronicity, and then, of course, how to reply and summon the courage to do so.

(My Soul) A prerequisite to understanding our language is knowing that everything that has and ever will happen *to* you (in your terms) happens so that you may realize who you have always been, which many of your readers will take to mean becoming a better and higher version of their personalities. Therefore, in reality, there are no "this means we were meant to be together forever" prophecies, at least not in the manner they hope.

The reason for everything is to expand you and the entire universe in sympathy with the pursuit of your dreams.

This does not mean you can't have what you want. When your desires reach the level of choices, or even better yet realities, you are experiencing love at the highest level.

(LS) Okay, let's take this piece by piece, using a real-life situation. Let's say something happens, or someone says or does something that makes me feel inadequate, unworthy, or angry and resentful. What do I do next?

(My Soul) You know this very well.

(LS) I do, but I would love to hear you explain it to my readers, and maybe I can get something else from it, as well.

(My Soul) First, it needs to be made clear that we are going to be looking at things you all call negative, and we will be calling them your gifts, so that's important for you to know as we begin.

Everything is your gift, but only after it has already happened is it a gift that serves you.

I know this confuses most of you, and it's important to get it straight, first. I know you know this, but it might help if you play the role of a confused reader for everyone else here.

(LS) Deal. Confusion is my specialty. Here goes:

How can it be possible that the same thing you say is *negative* before it happens all of a sudden becomes *positive* after it happens?

(My Soul) I didn't say it was *negative*, I said that everything is your gift, but only after it has happened is it a gift that serves you.

This is the same as saying that every *present* is your *gift*.

The future is still your choice, but the present is always your gift.

That is, every present *moment* is your gift, and if you don't understand why yet, at least you need to understand all of the reasons to trust it. Reasons give beliefs strength. When you get to a place where you have zero regrets, that is when you can say you understand this. If you have done something you're not proud of, having no regrets does not mean you want to do it again.

"No regrets" simply means: I am happy with who I am today. I love who I am.

Who you are today is the sum of all your experiences, which include all of the things you're not proud of. So, being happy with who you are today means you have no regrets. Also, the only time you can regret anything is when you are not connected to us.

(LS) I love what you're saying about regret here, and you've communicated it in a way I can readily understand, but I don't get what you mean when you say that, when we regret, we are not connected to you. Please explain.

(My Soul) Whenever anyone regrets something, think of their reasons for doing so. You said something or did something and you didn't get the job or you didn't get the relationship; or you didn't win the competition and you regret not training sufficiently. Every possible reason for regret is all about *what you missed out on*. When you are aligned with us, regret is not possible, because everything is designed to take you higher, make you more, get you to realize who you are. When you are connected and aligned with us, what you *missed out* on becomes your greatest gift, because you finally realize that without missing out on it, you would have missed out on so much more.

You look at what *you* missed out on, and *we* look at who you were awakened to because of what you missed out on.

You may not respond in a way that will make you realize who you really are immediately, but we know that eventually you must. Getting you to choose love is what this is all about. Getting you to respond in a way that will benefit everyone and everything is how we choose love in this situation, and this conversation will help people get there. Who you are is more important than anything you can have. Who you are is more valuable than any relationship, any job or business, and any competition. Who you are is about *us* (God, your heart, and I).

Who you are is about love, while *what you want* is about fear until you want it from a place of *choice* instead of *possibility*.

Come over to our side, for doing so is loving yourself and everyone else.

(LS) Wow! That was incredible. I really understand. I'm very happy that you said, "Who you are is more valuable than any relationship," because way too many people are focused on what they still call "mistakes" in their lives that they believe have cost them their happiness and even their identities, and it's the complete opposite, isn't that right?

(My Soul) Quite right, and this is why you should all celebrate everything.

Your "horrific mistake" is what makes your true identity possible, or more accurately, your response to it is what makes your true identity possible. Without both the mistake and your response, you prolong pretending and deny becoming.

(LS) And few know about that better than I do.

(My Soul) Your life is about what's real, and only love is real.

(LS) You know, you told me to play the part of a confused reader, so I ask questions I feel I know the answers to, and although I do understand the concept, I always learn much more every time you speak.

(My Soul) Everything is in levels. You do know the answers. All I'm doing is raising your awareness of how well you know the answers.

(LS) This is awe-inspiring. Oh my God, thank you! I think this could be the greatest book ever written, and yet there may be a possibility that someone tries to put me in a mental institution for writing it.

(My Soul) And that would be the greatest compliment you could ever receive.

(LS) Please don't get me started. I could probably go for hours on that one.

(My Soul) I'm being serious. There is not one person alive who does not have every answer they need. You know from experience that you cannot access knowledge that you don't believe you have, or even worse, knowledge you "know" you don't have. You are one who knows you have the answer, yet there are still things you don't access because you don't believe you can at a high enough level.

(LS) So, all of the people who sarcastically called me a "know it all" throughout my life were telling the truth about me and were lying about themselves?

(My Soul) Beautiful, but if they don't know they're lying, you may have to call it something else. You've got the idea.

(LS) Yes, definitely.

(My Soul) The universe is designed to make you want to strive for your desires. Let's take something you would understand but might find it difficult to agree with. Let's say you are walking across a busy street. You try as hard as you can to stay safe, but after trying really hard, you get hit by a car and end up in a hospital for three months.

(LS) Come on! Please! Are you really going to try to tell me that being hit by a car and confined to a hospital bed for three months is really a good thing?

(My Soul) Absolutely! Once it has already happened, what are your choices? You tell me what would serve you better "after" it has happened.

(LS) Oh, so what you're saying is that it's not really good; it's just the way you choose to see it after it happens, right?

(My Soul) Sorry, again. Only half right. The way you created it is the way it really is. You are in charge. When you believe it's not really good, but you pretend that it is, what are you doing?

(LS) Lying?

(My Soul) Exactly.

(LS) And isn't telling myself it's a good thing that I got hit by a car also lying?

(My Soul) I want to make sure everyone who reads this understands what I mean so your readers don't misunderstand this and run into the street, not caring if they get hit by a car, or worse, trying to get hit because "we" said it's good.

(LS) *We* did not say it's good, *you* did. I'm not sure what would benefit someone more, suing you or me.

(My Soul) Ha, gold diggers will want no part of me. The till is completely empty.

(LS) And mine is not exactly overflowing at the moment, but let's get back to business.

(My Soul) *If something painful has not happened yet, whether it is emotional pain or physical pain, do whatever you can to make it "not" happen.* Do not seek pain of any kind, but once it has already happened, that's when you get to choose what it is going to mean to you. There is nothing good or bad in absolute terms. There is only good or bad in *your* terms, and you get to choose your terms.

You never look at what has happened and judge it as good or bad, even when you think that's what you're doing. We look at what has happened and always *make* it good or bad. This is a fact, whether you believe it or not.

(LS) That is awesome. So, our "judgments," when we think that's what we're doing, usually make the situation the way everyone sees it?

(My Soul) Absolutely right, and always making the situation the way the judger sees it. You are not the only one who falls into the presupposition trap. When everyone you know sees a situation the same way and speaks and acts as if it's not possible for it to be any other way, it is hard for all of you to resist, and it's even harder when it's *your* situation or something you did.

(LS) This has been great. Tomorrow, let's talk about how people can recognize what you're saying based on the underlying knowledge that every one of your messages is designed to take us higher and how to connect to that power source through action.

(My Soul) Sounds like a plan. Why not tonight? Got a plane to catch?

(LS) If I could "catch" planes, I'd be working for Homeland Security.

(My Soul) Stick to writing. Go celebrate your halfway mark, and we'll talk tomorrow.

(LS) Deal.

GETTING HURT IS INEVITABLE

(MY SOUL) EVERY time you're hurt, it is an opportunity to grow or realize who you really are. It is part of a plan; it's inevitable. We wait to see what you're going to do and how you will respond. Will you choose love, or will you allow fear to delay love?

(LS) There must be more than just fear. Tell us why we don't take action even when we clearly feel the impulse to act?

(My Soul) I think everyone can relate to what it feels like when someone tells them they can't do something they say they are going to do.

(LS) Yes. It sets us on fire! We want to prove them wrong, so we work even harder, while dreaming of the day we can show them who we really are.

(My Soul) Exactly, and I chose this example for many reasons. One important reason is that it was something you had already said you were going to do. In this example, you were already planning to do something you were told you can't.

(LS) Then, how do we act on something we had *not* planned on doing or didn't know we were supposed to do?

(My Soul) This is where you put it all together by understanding the language of feeling, synchronicity, believing, and even *knowing* that you *can* do what we are telling you to do and then taking action.

A really important piece is figuring out what we're saying you should be doing. You will always respond to us through your actions, so it would have to be something that takes you higher, makes you more, or helps you grow or realize who you have always been. You need to know that no other response serves you. In the above example, you already knew what you wanted to do, and someone not believing in you spurred you to understand the message to "do what you've been told you can't or explode trying." It doesn't matter that you didn't know there was a message; the *feeling* made you want to accomplish your goal even more. And by the way, the "explode trying" part is a metaphor that you, for some reason, still seem to take literally.

The most important part of the energy that is given to you as a gift from someone you say doesn't believe in you is energy to realize who you have always been so as to accomplish what you've been told you cannot accomplish. This is extremely important, because this energy helps both you and me. Do you understand this?

(LS) Yes, I really do, but I have some questions. What do you mean by, "a gift from someone you say doesn't believe in you?"

(My Soul) No one has ever done anything *to* you, remember? Everything is meant to be *for* you, even those things that none of you understand. What was said or done was meant to be a gift, and everyone believes in you.

(LS) Come on, how can that be?

(My Soul) They don't remember that what they have done *to* you was something they had already agreed to do to help you. They have forgotten who they are and how much they love you and believe in you, and it would help everyone if you would remember not only who *they* are, but also you.

(LS) How can we know this is true? I'm not saying I don't believe you, but how can we verify this for ourselves?

(My Soul) There will come a time when you will not have to ask that question because you will know, without having to know *how* you know. In one of your favorite movies, *The Last Dragon*, the most important message the student receives from his master is: "When you know without knowing, you have touched the final level." Meaning that when you know without knowing *how* you know, you have reached what they call the final level.

(LS) Yes, I love that movie. Yet, there are so many things I thought I knew, I mean really *knew* I knew, that turned out not to be true.

(My Soul) Yes, I know that about you, but this is different. Love is not just what you think it is; love is responsible for everything beautiful, and when you choose what you want to be beautiful, you are choosing love. This is the perfect feeling of love that you have experienced in every beautiful moment of your life.

Love can be found in those unexplained experiences that you would have bet your life had nothing to do with love, for instance when you were running the hill, playing basketball, gazing into the eyes of the one you love, and writing with me. Love can be found in the things you consider insignificant, and they are only insignificant until you can't walk or talk anymore. Love is there whether you know I'm writing with you or not. Even when you were not consciously aware that I was writing with you, you were conscious of something, but you didn't know what it was. Love can be seen on anyone's face. Love can be seen interacting with the world. It's unmistakable. People can't stop smiling. No matter what anyone says or does, they can't be anything but ecstatic.

How would you like to have a life like that? Would you believe that it has been continually offered to you, but you keep refusing to accept it? Acceptance is not what you think it is, not even close.

Come on, I *know* you know this. Does love really cause you to be happy, or does being happy cause you to be in love? Love is an endless loop; it doesn't matter where you start. Smile, not just with your face, but with every thought, word, feeling, and action. Know that it doesn't matter one bit whether love caused you to be this happy or whether being happy caused you to be in love! Yes, love is kind of like a merry-go-round, and it doesn't matter where you get on or get off. If only you knew how close you are!

(LS) Yes, I get that, but how do we choose love when someone is trying to hurt us or we are in a situation that we don't know how to get out of? How do we choose love when we're completely lost?

(My Soul) This is exactly what we've been talking about: understanding how never to be lost again.

(LS) Okay, but there are still some things I don't understand here.

(My Soul) Love is there, and you don't have to know it. It will become visible to you when you get to a place where you truly believe you can do anything and when your actions reflect this. When you are armed with the belief and understanding that there is nothing you cannot accomplish, in your terms, you will no longer allow the pain from something someone said or some circumstance you find yourself in to stop you from acting, stop you from responding to our messages. You don't have to wait until you can believe you can do something, because there is always something you can believe in that will benefit you, everyone, and everything.

When you can't get yourself to believe you can do something, find something else you can believe in and act on that. Just make sure it moves you in the same direction of the original message.

(LS) What do you mean by "there is nothing you cannot accomplish, in your terms?"

(My Soul) *You still see many of your desires as not yet accomplished, while your heart and I live them without you until the rest of you awakens.*

(LS) Wow! That is so inspiring.

Okay, now we're getting there. I wish this were completely interactive so I could ask whether everyone else is with us.

(My Soul) Yes, people will have questions about it, but this is going to do more than you think it will. We are not only helping people out of pain, but also helping them make their dreams come true. And at the same time, we are expanding the entire universe in a way no one fully understands, yet, including you.

(LS) Yes, I get that, but I know some will still be lost. Getting anyone to believe something they don't already believe is not going to be easy. It's never been easy for me.

(My Soul) It is very simple once you understand the principles. This will be great for you, as well, because regardless of what you say, you don't believe anything is possible, yet. You believe things that few others do—until you don't, and then you hurt yourself. You do exactly what I say. You believe what you can believe. At times, you stretch some things you're not sure of, yet. This is not bad, at all; it is how you discover yourself.

Please understand. Of course, the more you can believe, the greater value you add not only to you, but to the entire universe. But you don't have to believe you can make this work. There will always be something on the way to the original message that you can believe in right now. Believe in what you can, and take this in stages.

(LS) Wow! I didn't even realize I was doing that.

(My Soul) Everyone has a different definition for what is possible and what is not.

Telling people that you have the solution and then asking

them to believe that anything is possible is not a solution to them. Can you see this?

(LS) I do, but I also think it's good for us to stretch ourselves.

(My Soul) I agree, but you don't want to lead everyone to experience the pain that you have, even if it prods them to grow and realize. There is a safer way to grow, and I'm hoping you will understand that, now. You have grown enormously, and you have learned how to deal with the pain, but if you continue doing what you've done, it will kill you.

(LS) Are you saying that I should have done something different?

(My Soul) Not at all. I am saying to get the message, now. What you have already done is perfect for who you are. You have stretched yourself to places no one has gone, which has caused you to learn things that no one else ever has, and now you can use your knowledge to help those who are in pain. You will have the opportunity to do this in a way that no one ever has. You are not just getting people out of pain; you are enhancing our mission for them, as well as becoming their partner in expanding the universe. You are doing all of this while helping them get what they want, to the degree they can believe in what they want, but we are telling you to lighten up on the self-inflicted pain, now.

(LS) Seriously, if this book doesn't sell even one copy, it will still be the best thing I ever did.

(My Soul) Your mother wants one. I think your one copy is in the bag.

(LS) Maybe I should have my mother sign a promissory note so I can give it to my publisher. I might need the thirty-cent advance on that one book I'm selling.

(My Soul) I wanted to see where you were going to take this. I hope your editor has a sense of humor. Your comedic Tourette gives this material unique character. Your humor is starting to grow on me.

(LS) Okay, okay, let's get back to being serious. I'm not sure what my readers are going to think of this. I'm certainly no Jim Carrey.

(My Soul) What are you worried about? Your mother will love it.

(LS) Where were we? I understood your message. From now on, I want to grow from pleasure instead of pain. I honestly think my life might depend on it, now.

How do we have faith when we have no evidence at all that what we want is even possible?

(My Soul) You don't need faith when all the evidence is shown to you. Faith is when you can't see, hear, or feel any evidence of what you want, and you still move toward it. You don't need faith when all the evidence is shown to you. The highest level of faith is knowing, and the highest level of knowing is the closest you can get to your heart.

(LS) Is this the reason that faith and knowing are the highest forms of love, because they're close to your heart?

(My Soul) Exactly.

Your heart *is* everything *you* desire. Contrary to everyone's beliefs, a heart has no desires, only realities. You are the one with the desires, while your heart lives them. Moving toward your heart, that is, following your heart means so much more than anyone ever knew.

When it comes to your heart, the opposite of what the world believes is true, and even many of your masters would disagree with this. The closer you get to your heart, the further away from your desires you will be and the closer to your realities.

A heart can only have what you call desires in terms of choices, making selections, but never in terms of hope, odds, or probability, unless it's the probability of a choice. The true meaning of "follow your heart" is to move to a place where all your dreams already are true; it's a vibrational place, an energetic place, a feeling place.

When you arrive at a place where you can't tell whether or not your dreams have come true, it's because they already have, even if they're not yet a physical reality. Focus is not merely observing reality; focus changes reality according to what you believe about what you're seeing. At this point, what you want is real to you in every dimension, and you are one with your heart. This is when you've found a type of love you never knew existed. This is how a love you never understood creates.

(LS) I had to read that over many times. Although I've been writing about this for years, I've never explained it this way. Thank you.

(My Soul) Well, you just explained it that way, now.

(LS) Touché.

Then, all the pain I have experienced is because of the distance between my heart and the rest of me on a vibrational and energetic level?

(My Soul) Yes, exactly, but it's not all bad. You experienced a lot of pain, but you also grew from experiences that few others have had the chance to.

(LS) I know there are many people that experience much more pain than I do.

(My Soul) Yes, and please stop trying to compete with them. There is a much smarter way to grow your beliefs without risking your life every time you do it.

(LS) I thought you said that everything that has happened is perfect.

(My Soul) It is perfect, and this is exactly why you are in a situation that has caused you to make so many necessary changes in your life; they are character changes that will last a lifetime. Do you see how perfect this is, how with our system you *must* continue on the path to authenticity, realization, and love. You can make it take longer, but you can never change it.

(LS) Yes, I do see that. I just wish it wouldn't take so long. From what you have been telling me, though, I know that the time it has taken is the best possible scenario for me, and shorter would not have been better, at least not in the past, right?

(My Soul) Exactly, now you're getting it.

(LS) Can you simplify what we've been talking about before we move on to our hearts and love?

(My Soul) Yes, good idea.

Every time you experience pain, an inspirational message is being delivered. At that moment, ask yourself, "If I can do anything, what would I do right now?" Now, if you're resentful and you want to get back at someone, this is not what I mean. I'm talking about something that would make you look better than you feel at that moment. Sometimes in the middle of drama and bad feelings, you need to wait until you can step back and find a way to love. And if you can't love someone else at this moment, find a way to love yourself. By loving yourself, I don't mean the vow to never give your heart completely again. This is a statement spoken by resentment, and it's valuable to be able to see that in yourself and others.

As you well know, being honest with yourself is not easy. Try to stay with me here, because this is not only life-changing for you, it moves the entire universe forward and can be a paradigm shift for your planet when it catches on. If you knew the impact of just one person converting heartache or any other kind of emotional pain into a huge blessing, you would all be teaching and learning this in your schools and life, making this world a better place. If we all had started this just five years ago, you would not recognize the world you live in today. I know this doesn't sound like love to you, but you would all love and be loved at a level you can't see right now, if you loved yourself in this way.

(LS) I have experienced it, and I know it's right, but please explain this so that my readers will know why it is true.

(My Soul) Sure. What could be more appropriate than to give the real-life example of how you became a writer and what that has already done for countless people.

If you want to create a miracle, love when no one would believe it's even possible.

You wrote your first line on May 4, 2010, and you started writing so that you could express how much you loved someone. Although love was not your first reaction, you eventually got to a place where all you wanted to do was love and, under the circumstances, it was not an easy thing to do.

(LS) I want to add something here. I don't know if this is correct or not, but I felt vulnerable when I got angry, and I felt I was being protected when I loved.

(My Soul) Beautiful. Yes, that's true, but let's not confuse everyone, because there are reasons that we can't go into right now.

(LS) Deal. Continue.

(My Soul) Exactly what the quote says is what happened. You found a way to love someone when no one would believe it was even possible, and you did this not for you, but for the person you loved. The result was what all of you would call a miracle. Look at how many people's lives have been touched because of your conversion of pain to love. Most people would say, "You want me to love, but look at what was done to me." Love does not mean you disrespect yourself or accept from anyone something you know you never should, because that would not be love. Love always means that everyone wins. And the truth is, I don't want you to love if it's not real; in fact, it is impossible to love if it's not real. If you don't feel it, it is a whole lot better to move on than to fake it.

No love has ever been fake, and no love ever will be.

Now, this is the impact of just one person, and there is an even greater impact that no one can see, which we spoke about earlier. Also, I suspect this may be only the beginning.

When you really love someone, it doesn't go away just because there was a fight or you got angry; so when the clouds clear, step back and see how you feel. If love is still there, so is your greatest opportunity. Even if it's not, however, you can still choose to love. I don't mean you should fake it, but you can always choose to treat a person with love. You can always find an appropriate way to love anyone if you really try.

(LS) Isn't it true that our greatest gifts come from the times when it was most difficult to love?

(My Soul) It is, which means that you, Mr. Love Story, have some huge, unclaimed gifts.

(LS) I know I do.

I still think your message is the hardest thing to understand and act on.

(My Soul) Yes, we are only interested in you getting the job or relationship or winning the competition to the degree that you are choosing love to get there. Sending an email about "us" to someone who has just rejected you is *not* choosing love. I'm talking about a relationship that has never been, not a couple that has been married, or was in a long term relationship.

(LS) Yes, this is exactly what I mean. It's not so clear-cut, and many can be hurting themselves and others by making the wrong decisions.

(My Soul) Yes, but every situation is different, and there is no way to solve everyone's situation here. You are just showing people what is possible.

(LS) I know that, but some people are going to try what we're talking about here, and they may hurt themselves even more by doing so.

(My Soul) No one can make a wrong decision, and no one can hurt themselves. Only the perception of that part of you that is not me still believes this. So, when people find themselves in a place where their decisions have not moved them forward, and maybe even backward, they will need help, and you are the only one who can help with this strategy. Even if they don't turn to you, don't you understand that those who you say you may have unintentionally hurt will be faced with either giving up or finding some way to become more in order to solve what they see as their problem?

(LS) Okay, but what if they just give up?

(My Soul) Even when they give up, your job is done, and done quite successfully. It then becomes my job to bring them new experiences that eventually will lead them to believe in themselves enough that they will, on their own, choose to act. This process continues until they choose love, a part of love that most people still don't know exists. You cannot continuously act on something you don't believe in , and acting on what you believe in is a higher form of love.

(LS) I think I understand, now. *When our desires reach the level of choices, or better yet, realities, we are experiencing love at the highest level,* because in order to do this, we must be the closest to our hearts. Is that correct?

(My Soul) Perfect. I have explained this already, but this is a great time to go into it completely. Love is always the highest level of faith, the highest level of *knowing*. This is yet another reason why I keep moving you toward your heart. We want you to understand that your truth is, there are no obstacles in your life. An obstacle is just something you see when you forget who you are or when you listen to those you still see as knowing better than you. And you only listen to others when you have not yet discovered who you are. You are the universe, and we have come to expand you. We have come to let you know that you are in fact *us*. The faster we can get you to realize that, the faster we can get you to your heart, and the faster and more completely we all will realize together. Does this make sense to you?

(LS) Yes, but can you tell us what we actually *do* to be where our heart is or to become a complete vibrational match to our heart? How exactly do we get close to our heart?

(My Soul) Of course. You see no gap, no space between where you are and where you *choose* to be. You think, talk, act, and feel, as you do, not "as if" you know you're there, but because you can't see it any other way. It's the same concept as dealing with the erroneous presuppositions of others, only this is not erroneous. Even the erroneous presuppositions of others become real when you live them. Who knows this better than you, for you were two different people in two different places?

(LS) That is very true.

How do we see no gap and no separation when it's right in our face? The one we love the most has just rejected us, or our account is overdrawn and the mortgage is due, or worse, late. Realistically, how do we think, talk, act, and feel that what we want most is true in the face of all this? I'm quite sure everyone wants to know.

(My Soul) It's a great question, but you're thinking in terms of intellect and logic, and that is not how this works. You get yourself to experience the feeling of what it's like to be real, and you act on that *truth*. When you meditate while visualizing and live that vision while remaining in the same alpha state as your meditation, what you would call the miraculous happens. Your world adjusts to the state you're living in, not *as if*, but *because*, it is all part of you. This is *always* happening, and it can't be stopped or paused. You feel comfortable making plans for things you previously didn't know we're even possible for you. Things like this are indications that what you created is now real, even though at this point everyone else can only see evidence to the contrary.

(LS) Oh, my God, that has happened to me! I remember looking in my phone for the contact information of a friend with whom I have not yet had any physical connection, forgetting that it's not a physical connection yet and is not in my phone at the moment.

(My Soul) I know this, as I have experienced it all with you.

(LS) I'm amazed. Knowing you are always with me makes me feel less alone.

How do we close the gap between our hearts and the rest of us—the parts of us that are not eternal—and make this feeling real when everything we see, feel, and hear in our world says the opposite? How can we act on that truth when we don't see it as true, at all? Of course, ultimately, I would love to know how we get to a place where what we have created is so real that we act, not *as if* it were here now, but *because* it is.

(My Soul) Such a beautifully worded question. Let's dig into this.

First, you need to understand why your desire is true so you can remain authentic, not fooling yourself or anyone else.

(LS) How do we do this? How can we understand why something is true when we don't even believe that it is—or worse, when all the evidence shows that it's not?

(My Soul) If you still believe that, then you don't have all the evidence. The desires that you see as not real are not real to you because you have no evidence procedure for seeing them as real. Therefore, a gap that isn't really there widens only in your perception and becomes your personally created reality. Do you see this?

(LS) I think you're starting to lose me, here.

(My Soul) Okay, this is a perfect time to get to prayer and affirmations, as the answer to what I'm talking about can be found there.

THE POWER OF PRAYER AND AFFIRMATION

THERE HAS NEVER been a prayer that has not delivered exactly what was asked for, and there has never been an affirmation that has not produced exactly what was affirmed.

(LS) Okay, you've told me this before, I get it and I absolutely love it, but how do you explain all of the people who have not received what they have asked for and affirmed?

(My Soul) They're saying the prayer and affirmation in the wrong language, and so it is misunderstood. Also, they begin to undo the prayer and affirmation the moment they "believe" that they are no longer asking or affirming.

(LS) What do you mean by, "the moment they believe that they are no longer asking or affirming?"

(My Soul) You all think that you set aside a time to pray or do affirmations, and yet, the prayer and affirmation are continuous. Every moment of life is your prayer and affirmation. Just because you choose to stop doesn't mean it ended. So, assuming you don't ask for the reverse of what you say you want, which is what most of you do almost all the time, but even if you get that part right, the moment you believe your prayer or affirmation is finished, actually it continues as you undo it. Are you understanding this?

(LS) But, this sounds exhausting! I have to be creating all the time?

(My Soul) You don't have to create intentionally, but whether you like it or not, you are creating all the time; so it's better that you know it is going on. When you pray for peace today and go out and buy a bomb shelter tomorrow, all I want you to know is that those are two opposing prayers.

(LS) My actions are prayers?

(My Soul) Exactly and inescapably. Every action contains a message of what you believe in, who you believe you are, and what you expect is coming; this is prayer and affirmation of the highest order, and every one of these beliefs has levels of intensity. The degree of intensity either confirms or blurs the outcome. A vibration that is not completely certain gives you an uncertain result, and of course, complete certainty gives you exactly what you know to be true, providing that you really do know and are not just attempting to know.

(LS) And that last part explains why we get caught off guard?

(My Soul) There are times when we have convinced ourselves that we know, but we really never did. Yes, exactly.

(LS) I have been there many times. It was as if I wanted something to be true that wasn't, and so I was avoiding the truth and hoping by doing so that what I wanted to be true would somehow show up.

(My Soul) You can never create something that's not real. Avoiding the truth was an action of a lack of faith, which caused the opposite of what you wanted to be "realized." Are you making the connections, now?

(LS) Yes, yes of course. Thank you. I was trying too hard to accomplish what I wanted.

(My Soul) We do not *try* to accomplish something; we use the tools of creation to make a *selection*, not to take a chance, and *everything* that happens helps us in this endeavor. Don't you see that we are accomplishing the same thing here?

Your world is a candy store, and every moment you are choosing your flavor.

(LS) Sometimes I get so caught up in my own production that I forget what's real and what matters.

Now, can you believe that every prayer and every affirmation that was ever made since the beginning of time has delivered exactly what was asked for, without fail?

(LS) Yes, but I know people will have a difficult time with this, so please clarify it for all of us.

(My Soul) Sure. Every word of the quote above is absolutely true. I know this doesn't sound like it can be true, and I'm sure you can point to many prayers of yours that have not been answered, but they have, and I completely understand why you think they have not, so please allow me to explain.

(LS) Sure, please.

(My Soul) Again, I'm going to need you to play the role of a reader who doesn't quite get this, yet, so you can ask what they would want to know.

(LS) I'm there.

(My Soul) First, you need to understand what you're asking for in *our* terms.

(LS) What do you mean? What are your terms?

(My Soul) Many of you think that prayers to God are the same as kids' letters to Santa Claus: "If I'm really good, God is going to see this and reward me by answering my prayers." Nothing can be further from the truth.

(LS) Come on, you know this is not going to sit well with some people.

(My Soul) I cannot be responsible for how, or even where, anyone sits. You can build a house in church and your prayers will still not be answered because of that.

(LS) But why? Doesn't God want us to be good and follow Him?

(My Soul) Yes, of course, but not because you will be rewarded if you do. God designed your adventure to authenticity. Using a carrot-and-stick approach to "train" you, or giving you a "treat" for good behavior, as if you were Fido, makes a mockery of God and does not serve His purpose for you.

(LS) Okay, I can understand that, but what about those who go to church every Sunday so that they will go to their "reward."

(My Soul) Don't you understand that we want you to make a higher decision, not one you make because you are going to be given something? You are all on a journey to authenticity that God designed. Rewards and punishments render all of your actions counterfeit.

Your *reasons* for doing what you do mean everything. It's the difference between loving someone because you really do love them and loving someone because you are being paid in some way to do it, which is *not* loving them. When you love someone because you believe you will be rewarded, it is as fake as if you are being paid to love someone. Does this make sense to you?

(LS) It sure does make sense to me, but there will still be those who say, "God is higher than us. God is above us, and so He can do whatever he wants to.

(My Soul) Okay, I don't want to get too far off the subject and into a discussion about hierarchy, so let's just say that God is higher than you. Why then would He want to give all of you the example of "lowering" His standards? Why would God pretend or try to be something less? Answer these questions for yourself and see if they make any sense to you.

(LS) I think you made your point, and I surely agree. I have always believed that God is higher than the way most of us see Him.

Let's get back to where we were. If we are not punished or

rewarded, and if it really is true that every prayer and affirmation has and always will deliver exactly what is being requested, what's the secret? What are we not getting about this?

(My Soul) Your prayer or affirmation travels through what you call the empty space in front of you. The words you say to this "empty space" have no effect or direction, at all. The only part your words play in your prayer are their ability to get you to believe that you already have what you are praying will come.

(LS) This doesn't make any sense. Why would we pray to receive something that we already have?

(My Soul) Exactly!

(LS) Huh?

(My Soul) I'm not joking. You completely uncovered it.

(LS) Well, I have no idea what you're talking about or what you say I've uncovered.

(My Soul) Every prayer and affirmation is answered immediately, and every answer will always be *the place* from which they were sent.

(LS) I don't get it. What do you mean *the place?*

(My Soul) When you pray for something you don't have or you affirm something with the hope of receiving it, these requests are delivered from a *place* of not having what you hope to soon receive. So, without knowing it, you are really asking to receive more of not having what you say you want. Do you get this?

(LS) Wow! This is incredible, but I have a question. Why make it so difficult? Why not just permit us to ask in the language that we understand?

(My Soul) You *are* permitted to ask in the language you understand. You can also say "Abracadabra," but neither one will get you where you want to go. Our mission for you is the reason that what you want is not just handed to you. This system is designed to get you closer to your heart, where, as we said earlier, there are no desires, but only realities. Being closer to your heart means being closer to love and closer to God. Giving you what your words are asking for without you having to become something more robs you of your true identity and denies you the gift of love and God. If anyone walking the earth should know this, it should be you. It is the very reason this conversation started. It is, in part, why Byron Katie's *The Work* turned into a real conversation for you.

(LS) Wow!

(My Soul) My mission in your life is to do everything I can to make you more, to prod you to remember, uncover, and ultimately realize who you really are. I use people, places, circumstances, and events to deliver the appropriate messages in the form of *feeling*. These messages are personalized for you; they are intended to help you to feel deep inside of me, deep inside your soul. These inspirational messages are intended to prompt you to respond in action. In order for you to do this, you must move closer to your heart, to love, to me, and to God.

(LS) There seems to be a lot of confusion about what it means to be closer to our hearts, to love, to you, and to God.

(My Soul) Yes, there sure is. This may be more misunderstood than anything we've ever written about. Your heart is the bridge that connects both worlds, but neither I nor God reside in a physical place, so to be closer to us is an emotional journey. The *feeling* is not easy to describe in words. The closest I can come to describing it is to say that it is the most incredibly beautiful feeling of peace, love, and vibrational/ energetic certainty.

(LS) You need to simplify this. Explain what you're saying in one sentence.

(My Soul) Live as close to the world that we—the non-physical part of your heart, me, and God—live in, while still remaining physical.

This is your one sentence. I realize that there will be some questions about this, such as what is different about the world we live in. The world I live in with my roommates—your heart and God—has no obstacles.

(LS) How can this even be possible for us to do? Where and how do we start?

(My Soul) Do you remember that we started this topic by saying that every prayer and affirmation ever made since the beginning of time has delivered exactly what was asked for every time without fail?

(LS) Yes, absolutely. I've been wondering when you were going to get back to it.

(My Soul) If, as I say, the statement is really true, can you imagine what it means for your life and your future?

(LS) I've been thinking about it every day since we wrote it. I know it's true. I don't have to ask; I can feel it.

When I'm connected, I can feel the universe moving in my favor, *as if* it is part of my circulatory system, nourishing my galaxies. Or should I say, *because* it is?

It's like I've been asleep for fifty years and just now woke up.

This is the closest I have ever come to communicating this truth. It is a beautiful feeling, and it now makes sense to me that this is part of love. What releases the most resistance for me is the thought that we are always asking, and whatever we are asking for, it's impossible not to get.

(My Soul) Beautiful. This is what I mean by living in our world while still remaining physical. You just gave us a perfect example of it. Thank you for sharing. I know not everyone will believe this at first, but the moment your readers become aware of what they're asking for and know why and how they're asking, it will all become clear.

(LS) No, thank *you*. I would love to see that happen. I can't even imagine how much peace it would give so many.

(My Soul) Now, imagine if you actually understood how

much of what you would call one person's failed attempt, does for everyone and everything.

(LS) I don't think too many have more of those than I do.

(My Soul) So that you can understand how I feel when you make a statement like that, think of your daughter calling and telling you that she is feeling down because things are not coming together in the manner and the time that she wants. Your message to her is becoming my message to you, right now. If you could see what I see from where I am, you would know you have nothing to worry about. You know what you're doing right, and you know what you're not doing. You are right on target, and you can't possibly make a wrong decision. Does any of this sound familiar to you?

(LS) Yes, only modified a little. Thank you. I hope my kids learn from this, although I feel I may have a lot less credibility with them after they read this.

(My Soul) Why would you affirm or pray to have less credibility with them?

(LS) Wow! Touché. Thank you!

(My Soul) No worries. Soon, it will feel natural to know that everything you think, say, and do is a creation, and that everything that happens, happens to help you realize who you have always been.

(LS) I know it. I just get caught up in life and forget who I am—who we *all* are.

Let's get back to prayers and affirmations. This is a fascinating subject for me. It's going to be difficult for everyone to believe that we are extremely close to everything we have ever wanted.

(My Soul) And that is only because you don't know who you are yet, and I mean *all* of you. When you really know who you are, you'll never have another day like today; you'll never feel down because someone doesn't believe in you at the level you think they should.

(LS) I'm very much looking forward to that day.

(My Soul) It's an every, "right now" choice. It is like speaking a new language. You know the language, but you just have to remember to speak it often enough that it becomes as natural as speaking what you call your native language, until it becomes as natural as walking and doing all you do without thinking. And please don't forget that every action speaks, so be aware of what you are saying, asking and bringing into your life. Prayers and affirmations can only be "delivered" in the language of feeling. The only value in your choice of words is their effect on how you feel. English, German, French, Spanish, or whatever you were born speaking is *not* your first language.

(LS) I always thought that our words go out into the universe and create, maybe on a more basic level than feelings and actions, but they create nonetheless.

(My Soul) And you were right about that, because every thought, word, and action is responsible for a feeling. There is no prayer or affirmation that is spoken *only* in words. They are always spoken in thoughts, words, feelings, and actions. Every feeling has a *place* of origin, and every thought, word, and action has an origin, as well. The birthplace of every thought, word, feeling, and action, unlike our own birthplace, is not set in stone. As we change the origin of any of these four elements, we change their realities, and they change ours.

Each one of these four elements of creation has its own realities built into it. Every answer you get will always be the *place* from which the prayer or affirmation was sent. The prayer, "Please, God, cure my cancer" can only come from a *place* of having cancer, so to the universe or God, this is a request to "continue having" cancer. Now a prayer or affirmation that says, "Thank you God for curing me," must come from a *place* of already being cured. Please be aware that your words are not all that is speaking, and that you don't undo the prayer after you say the prayer is over.

Are you grasping this? Can you see from what I'm saying here how you can get your thoughts, words, feelings, and actions to come from the *place* of your greatest dreams being true, right now? When you do this, every prayer becomes one of gratitude.

(LS) Yes, I do see that, but I don't understand why we are required to communicate in this way in order to get the result we want. I have a hard time believing that God does not understand what I want.

(My Soul) When you start thinking in terms of your higher purpose, you will no longer ask such questions. Of course, God knows what you really want. We all know what you really want, but it does not serve our purpose or yours to *give* you what you want. You must understand that you don't realize who you are when we give you what you want. You only realize who you are by not remembering who you are and putting it all back together yourself. To ask in the way we want you to ask, you have to *realize* (make real and display as real) who you already are. You must *become* who you already are all over again. Do you understand? Do you understand why, now?

(LS) Yes, I do understand. I just keep forgetting it.

(My Soul) Reasons and manner are everything. It's not merely what the actions are, but *how* you take them that speaks. It's not just what the words are, but how you speak them that determines where your words come from. Are you speaking as if you believe what you're saying with every fiber of your being, or are you and your cells rolling your eyes as you say what you obviously do not believe? Pretense has no power, because there will always be a part of you that knows you are pretending. Love is complete authenticity which makes both inescapable. Ultimately, every part of you must be on board. If you say, "Thank you for bringing wealth into my life," it doesn't matter what words you use if every cell in your body is screaming, "BS!" You've got to reach complete congruency.

If you really want what you want, you must learn to negotiate complete acceptance, realization, and knowing, not with anyone else, but with every part of *you*. Every request would, without fail, be delivered appropriately, but you have to understand and follow through on the entire process. Remember what I said earlier, that words alone are not enough? You must think, talk, act, and feel, not *as if,* but *because* you already have whatever it is you are choosing and *not* just during what we call the prayer, or affirmation, but every moment after that. Your entire life lived is the prayer and affirmation, and you can't press Stop, or even Pause; it is forever working.

Yes, you will see this as the daunting part, maybe a bit overwhelming, but you are already doing it. And now that you are aware that you are doing it, you can choose what you want in every moment. In fact, you *are* choosing what you want in every moment and you always have been, only now you know it. Every thought, word, feeling, and action also comes from a *place*, and you can now get them all to come from whatever it is you want. You can choose to have your thoughts, words, feelings, and actions reborn from a new *place*.

The importance of thoughts, words, feelings, and actions is not just what you're thinking, but *how* you think; not just what you say, but *how* you say it; not just what you feel, but *how* you feel it; and not just the actions you take, but *how* you take them. Every thought that you think including the *way* in which you think it has its own message to the universe. This message is telling the universe what to bring you, what will happen *for* you, and even when it will happen, but to say that thoughts alone create your world would be the same as saying that one ingredient makes up an entire cake.

Thoughts do become things, but only when your words,

actions, and feelings agree. Every word you speak has its own message to the universe, and most of the time, the message is completely independent of what you're trying to say or even what you think you're saying. There is never a moment that you are not speaking it. There is never a moment when you're not asking. And there is never a moment when you are not being given *exactly* what you ask for. God, the Universe, Source Energy, Infinite Intelligence—whatever you feel comfortable calling this power—has *always* given you exactly what you asked for, and it always will.

I can hear some of you saying, "It sure has not given me what I have asked for." Where do the words, "It sure has not given me what I have asked for" come from? They can *only* come from a *place* of not getting what you asked for, and when every part of you joins in to speak this along with your words, it becomes impossible to get what you think you have been asking for. Is this starting to make sense to you? Can you really know what you're asking for without understanding the language?

(LS) Yes, and as I said before, my only challenge is keeping it.

I think it would help to explain exactly what it means to live our lives from the place of being and having all we want. What do we do, and how exactly do we do it?

(My Soul) Where is the *place* you are living your life from, now? Are you living your life from a place of not being sure about what you want from life, or does every thought word and action reflect that what you want is already yours? Living your life from a place where everything already is yours is the most amazing feeling on earth. It comes from true knowing and not from an attempt to create any result.

(LS) I am mostly living from not being sure, but I have been aware of it for a long time and have gotten much better. I do have some questions about this. How do we continue to live from the place of being successful in whatever it is we want most when an expert in our field says they don't believe in us? And maybe they don't even say those words, but it sounds like that to us? I have had a hard time with this in the past.

(My Soul) Don't think for a second that the way you feel is not by design. The person who you say made you feel that way was part of a plan, along with you and *us*, so that you can, in your terms, become more—and in our world, realize who you always have been. Yes, this takes strength, but why waste another second? Why not start now?

Right now, visualize how you would look going through life relating to everyone you now relate to, only doing it from a *place* of the *you* who knows it has everything. As you see this picture of you, feel what it would be like and connect to this energy source. We all want to know when it will be our turn, right? We all want to know when our day will come. We all ask this question every day, if not in words, then surely in thoughts and actions. Do you remember what we wrote?

There isn't one person walking this planet who would not want to choose their own prayer or affirmation and have it come true. Those who completely understand this know that we not only *can* do this, but there *never* has and *never* will be a moment in our lives when we are *not* doing this. —Love Story

(LS) Yes, I remember when we wrote that. It is like being given the key to everything in life when we understand that we really can choose.

There is a question that had been bothering me for many years, and I've heard many others ask the same question. You gave me the most beautiful answer, and I want to share that here. I have heard this question asked of the most influential spiritual leaders, most of whom I have learned from and respect. Ironically, I got the answer from you while studying their material, although I have never heard what I believe to be an appropriate response or answer to this specific question before you gave it to me.

The question was this: I can flow the energy; I can match the vibration of what I want. I know I'm going to get it. I can feel it in my bones. But when is it going to show up? How long do I have to wait?

The answer I received from you was this: Any question you have about when something will arrive can only come from a *place* of not having it, and so with your question, you are now blocking the very thing you so successfully started creating when you were matching the vibration in the first place.

(My Soul) Yes, that is perfect. It is like having the key to life. Of course, I remember giving you that answer, but we're not done with this subject, yet.

(LS) Deal. Don't let me stop you.

(My Soul) The thought, "I'd better look for another job before I get fired," is like asking the universe to get your boss to fire you.

Now, you can tell me about the times you did something like this and *didn't* get fired. There are many valid reasons for this. It takes time and consistent patterns of thoughts, words, feelings, and actions to create something. Also, you may simultaneously know that you do a great job at work and that your boss really values and respects you. These conflicting patterns offset each other, and the most dominant is what will eventually become an experience. What causes one result to appear instead of another are time, intensity, emanation (where your thoughts, words, feelings, and actions are coming from), and authenticity.

These are all things that we not only can influence but also control through discipline. We can choose to spend more time and more intensity in the patterns that serve us. We can choose where our thoughts, words, feelings, and actions emanate from, and with practice, we can make it real. We don't have to allow patterns to take shape that will lead us to where we don't want to go. You can look at someone and very clearly determine, by the tone, speed, and volume of their voice, along with how they're carrying themselves, whether they are about to set the world on fire or have their entire life repossessed!

Okay, well, maybe everyone's life is not as volatile as yours has been, so it might be something in between. Your life has been on both extremes of these examples, but for most people, it's not as easy to tell where they are headed. This is not as easy as changing the way you walk and talk and then everything just falls into your lap. Faking it until you make it can work temporarily, but it usually doesn't stick, because who you *really* are always comes back. Even neurolinguistic programming (NLP) only works when it leads you to realize that you really *are* this successful and happy person, otherwise, you make temporary progress and revert right back. Tony Robbins can surely tell you about that. Changing the way you move and speak will feel great, but if that's all you do, it won't last.

This brings up a great point, because we are *not* trying to manifest anything, and even when we are, it would serve us not to do so. Only those who don't have what they want would possibly try to get it, and they can only get it from a place of not having it. You are, instead, growing into the realization that you already are who you want to be and already have what you say you want.

(LS) This is where you lose me, and I honestly believe that this is where you lose everyone. How do you expect anyone to believe that they are already wealthy when they can't even pay their phone bill? I can tell you that they don't feel wealthy, and their reality is much different from the reality you see for them.

(My Soul) And that is exactly why they are in *their* reality; in that moment, they can see only "who they are not."

(LS) Can't you understand why they feel the way they do?

By the way, I have been there. I remember when I couldn't pay my own phone bill.

(My Soul) It was supposed to happen and of course I understand why they feel the way they do, I made it that way. Everyone needs something to grow out of, in your terms. This is how you realize who you are, and the universe expands simultaneously.

(LS) Please, don't give me anything more to grow from. I have enough now to be growing for a million lifetimes.

You say that we all need something to grow out of, but when we get buried under more than we can handle, how does it serve us to just give up because we don't believe we can handle it all? I mean, isn't there a simpler way to explain this so people can say, "If I just do these three things today, I'll be great?" Or, better yet, one thing? I know this is not a simple subject, but come on; you're sporting the energy of God for "someone else's" sake.

(My Soul) You need to have faith and trust that I might know what I'm doing. You need to get yourself to a place where you feel the release of resistance and then you will have more faith and trust.

(LS) That is not exactly the answer I was looking for.

(My Soul) When you know exactly what answer you're looking for, there is no need to ask, or even look for that matter.

(LS) I walked right into that one.

(My Soul) I understand you perfectly, but not everyone feels release from the same words; and feeling the release is what is really important. I put together some short quotes along with some long explanations so your readers can discover what triggers the release for them.

(LS) Okay, our ears are yours—and also our hearts, by the way.

(My Soul) Beautiful, thank you.

The feeling is authentic when your focus creates it instead

of you manufacturing it. All you need to do for it to continue is to maintain focus. The focus creates the feeling, and the feeling produces the actions without you having to act artificially. This is an endless loop. Motion does create emotion, as well, but if that is all you do, it won't stick. Maintaining focus on one truth will make this easier and less confusing, and it will help the feeling last, as you will soon see.

(LS) I really want to hear about how to make the feeling stick.

(My Soul) There is a great deal to this, but it sounds more difficult to achieve than it really is. The good news is that you don't have to remember all of this; you just have to practice doing one thing really well. You will eventually come to know what causes you to feel the release of all resistance, and you can focus on that. You will eventually learn to get every part of you to go directly to *knowing,* and you'll discover that it's important enough to do whatever it takes to get there.

Every part of you is always speaking; every thought, word, and action has a message. You don't have to constantly be thinking about what every movement is saying, but it will help if you're aware of what you're asking and affirming. The state of faith or knowing will move you without your having to think about moving.

This is it. This is all you have to do. Everything you need will flow from here. All of the rest takes care of itself. The four ingredients of creation—thoughts, words, feelings, and actions—all arise from your focus. When you live your life from the *place* of knowing that everything you *choose* is already done, then it must be, and the only possible way to change it is to focus on what your world is like when you don't get what you want. When you live your life from *knowing,* then everything is a choice, a selection, and already yours! When you live from fear, doubt, and worry, you *want* things because you don't have them and don't have choices, just hope that you will get what you want someday.

Are you understanding this? Does it make sense to you? Practice turning this on at will, and then, ultimately, live life this way. Being who your heart is right now comes from *knowing*. Own what your heart and I own, and live the life your heart and I are living right this second. Then, you won't have to wait for anything you want. Going directly to *knowing* is living the life of your heart and me, and this you can do right now. Everyone's beliefs about this subject are visible and completely transparent. No one can hide or be untruthful about it without everyone who understands knowing the truth. Where you are right now is exactly what you have affirmed, exactly what you have prayed for. You *chose* the prayer. Exactly where you are right now is exactly what you *decided* to pray for or affirm.

Maybe, you didn't know you were deciding it. These choices are not conscious, and so they go completely unrecognized; and yet, they are still choices. Just the awareness and understanding that this is true will take your journey of realization to a beautiful place, a place where you have control. You always had control, but you just never knew it. Now that you know it, you know how important is it for *you* to consciously choose and to be aware of what you're choosing. Imagine life after mastering this! On this subject, even the most evolved and enlightened still limit their prayers and affirmations because of what they believe.

The choice to believe in something you want to happen is a choice to move closer to your heart, and because you *want* it to happen, you are not there yet. Even so, it is a start. When I use the word *want* here, I'm using it in the sense of desiring something, that you don't yet have. To accomplish this at the highest level is to live from your heart, which is a feeling of almost complete weightlessness because you are living life from the non-physical. It feels like heaven on earth for a very good reason—it is.

Coordinate your partners of thought, word, feeling, and action to come from your heart, the only place where all your dreams are already true. You can't even argue with this. Divine intelligence created this system so that every argument against it helps to prove it right. How would *I* know every argument against this proves it right? When someone says, "I've tried this and it never works," where does "it never works" come from? "It never works" can come only from a place of it not working. So, what you will get is "it not working." Even "it never works" is proof that it does work.

Every cell in every part of your body takes its direction from your every communication. They obediently wait for your orders. No one knows how many cells are in our bodies; the estimates I've heard range from 100 billion to 100 trillion. Think of it: you have complete command of, possibly 100 trillion co-creators of everything in your world, and they all work perfectly together to create whatever you ask, every time. So, do you know what you've been asking for? Can you really be completely sure you know? Using the right words are only important to the degree that they get you and your 100 trillion cells to dance to the rhythm of your heart's realities.

The universe is a playground that God created for all of his children, and if His children want to have a lot of fun in this playground, there are some realities that it would serve them to know. As a child in this playground, you can have anything you choose, but nothing you want. The definitions of *want* and *choose* are not what's most important here; only what you perceive that these words mean to you has any significance.

The word *choose* comes from a place of already having whatever it is you're *deciding*. In other words, the buffet is yours; please take what you *choose*. The word *want* is usually associated with something we don't have but would like to have. However, at times, people use the word *want* when they really mean choose, and so they get the results of making a *selection* that they see as already theirs. In the creation process, the words alone mean nothing until they make you feel a certain way.

The feeling of wanting something that is not yours when you don't know how, or even if you will ever get it widens the gap between you and your heart, love, and God, and they are one and the same. Of all the connections to the universe, the heart's connection is the most unique. No heart will ever have the capability to see or feel any gap between a desire and a reality, and on the day that we *lose* this *disability*, we too will walk on water. To say that we have clarity when we are "realistic" about how far we currently are from our desires is always true because our limited vision makes this real to us.

The way we see things is always authentically accurate to us only, as our perception creates our reality. But we don't have to see them that way. We have been given the gift of free choice, which means many, many things, but on this subject, it means that we can see anything in any way we choose. We can authentically believe anything we choose, and we can feel any way we choose. This is the freedom to change your life and your world in a nano-second. Sorry—serious miscalculation; no wonder I could never pass any math classes. Once you fully get this, it doesn't take *any* time to change whatever it is you want to change. The only obstacle you have to living it now is believing it is true; but hang on, we're getting to that.

First, I want you to experience the feeling. Imagine you just won the lottery of life, and everything you have ever dreamed of is already yours. You haven't turned in your ticket, yet, but you know that as soon as you do, everything you want is all yours. And you turn in your ticket by getting 100 trillion crusaders to dance to the reality of your heart, but you must lead the way.

You must start dancing, first. Once you start playing around with this, it is easy to determine what you're saying, what you're asking for, and what you are affirming.

I know it sounds like a lot to remember, and I want you to know that you don't have to try to remember anything. This is all knowledge that we already possess, but our focus on physical life has distracted us from it.

I want you to experience this feeling at the highest level at least once, because once is all you need to never want to let it go. As you experience this feeling, every worry disappears and every challenge is already accomplished; you feel so incredible that I will not even try to describe it, because I don't believe I could even touch the surface. Sorry, but you will have to get there to know what I'm talking about. My goal right now in this chapter is to simplify the process for you.

The author Gregg Braden has done some really incredible work on the heart in terms of creating and manifestation. He has said, "The feeling is the prayer." Just as important as the feeling is where the feeling comes from and how it is generated. When feeling is manufactured artificially, it's kind of like that phrase, "Fake it until you make it." The cells in your body play a huge part in this, and they will know that you're faking it.

Now, there may be times when your cells are asleep and they start to believe that the artificially manufactured feelings and words are real. So, "fake it until you make it" can work temporarily, but eventually you always go back to who you really are. I know this is a lot to absorb, but please understand what we're trying to accomplish here. Think about the truth; think about what's possible, or better yet, think about what's already real. This is like being given a magic crystal, and all you have to do is learn how to use it.

Your heart is a liquid crystal oscillator that is at the heart (yes, pun intended) of everything you have ever created and everything you ever will.

I'm going to simplify this for you, I promise. You want feeling that comes from your focus on understanding realization and *knowing*. Artificially manufactured feelings feel great, but they don't last, and there are times when you will be able to tell that the feelings have no direction. When this happens, you can instantly know where they *didn't* come from.

Understanding this entire philosophy will be helpful, so read this chapter over and over. Make a study of it. Instead of just reading the book once and putting it down, read it through and study it regularly. This is what you did with the books you learned from. You read them through and studied them daily for about thirty-eight years.

Ultimately, you will reach the point where the amazing feeling of *knowing* comes from focus. It is valuable to experience the contrast between feeling that arises from a reason and feeling that is manufactured. Initially, you may not be able to get to this feeling from knowing, and so you have to begin with an artificially generated feeling.

I urge you to do anything it takes to learn the difference between authentic and artificially generated feelings, even if you have to take a Yoga Nidra class, a yoga that can help you experience this feeling. Even if you need to travel across the country to take a class, do it. It is really that valuable.

There was a lot in this explanation, so let's do a little recap. The answer to every prayer and affirmation will always be the *place* from which it was sent. If your prayer is a request like requests in the physical world, you will always be disappointed unless your belief, or better yet, your knowing is strong enough to override it. If you ask your neighbor, "May I please have a cup of sugar?" Your neighbor will certainly understand, but the same request to the universe will keep you in a state without sugar.

To God, the Universe, Source Energy, or Infinite Intelligence, "May I please have a cup of sugar?" must emanate from a place of not having sugar, so not having sugar is what you get. Every thought, word, feeling, and action has its own reality, and this reality is also determined by the *place* from which it originated.

Understanding this entire philosophy is super-important, because it will prepare you to go directly to *knowing* more quickly. You will understand that you don't need to accomplish anything, that everything already is yours and all you need to do is *realize* it. Realizing it means, becoming aware that it is true and displaying this truth in every thought, word, feeling, and action.

It takes practice and some coordination, but it's just like walking; eventually we all get it, so don't give up. Live with your greatest problem already solved; live your most valued dreams, right now. Don't just fake it; *know*; know your dreams are true, now. If it feels like a lie to you, then start from something that doesn't feel like a lie and slowly move back to *knowing* again. You will know when you're faking it, and you just need to practice making it real. Faking it is not all bad. It teaches you how to feel and, ultimately, how to emanate the authentic feeling.

Never make a list of all the things you don't want, even if it's to create a strategy to avoid them. *Do not ever* work on correcting faults. Any action of correcting faults will always bring more of them into your life.

While working on yourself, *do not* search for faults to be corrected. Searching for what you don't want will bring you *more* of what you don't want. Instead, focus on who you want to become. Focusing on who you want to become will take you where you want to go and correct what you call your faults without drawing them to you.

Focusing on what you don't want is asking to have it brought into your life, even if you are very clear that you are asking them *not* to appear.

Create without caring about, or paying any attention to, any physical results at all. Your pleasure and reward should be in the love of creating, not in what comes after. So, not caring what manifests in the physical is the only way to be sure you get every physical thing you have ever wanted.

(LS) When you say, "not caring," you mean the emotional attachment to caring, right?

(My Soul) Yes, exactly. The emotional attachment to a physical result.

Once you create, know it is created and don't even consider the possibility of anything else.

(LS) Every time I read that statement, I feel intense peace and knowing. I feel almost completely weightless, as if I were floating. I wonder if any of my readers get that same feeling.

(My Soul) That feeling is your connection to us.

(LS) Many times while writing this book, I have felt that weightlessness, and I am still waiting for the day it never goes away. I'm not looking for my physical demise, just looking to keep that feeling and never have it leave while remaining in my physical body.

(My Soul) There are many disciplines you need to achieve before you can get closer to that.

(LS) I don't even have to ask what they are; I can *feel* the answer. This is very beautiful.

(My Soul) The prayer never ends, and the affirmation continues indefinitely. Every moment, every part of you is asking for something, and every moment you are receiving exactly what you are asking for. It can be no other way. You ask by being and living the life you know is yours or must eventually come.

What are you asking for, right now? What are you affirming this very second? Whatever it is, **you will never *not* get it.**

A HEART CAN NEVER BREAK

YOU HAVE TOLD me that a heart never breaks, and we have written about it. I thought this would be a perfect segue to what we were just talking about. Can you tell me why it is true?

(My Soul) Your heart is pure, positive energy, and here I am talking about the non-physical part of your heart. Your heart and I are what you will become when you die, in your terms. As I mentioned earlier, your heart has desires only in terms of choices, never in terms of possibilities.

(LS) What do you mean when you say I will become you and my heart when I die?

(My Soul) You don't die any more than water dies after it rains and the sun comes out.

(LS) Are you now saying that we evaporate?

(My Soul) I'm saying that, like water, you change form, and changing form is not dying.

Dying is not about sleeping forever; dying is when you are forced to wake up to what you never understood when you thought you were awake.

(LS) That is awesome. Thank you.

(My Soul) What you call dying is when you become the stuff that I and your heart are made of, the non-physical part of your heart, that is. When what you call dying occurs, you do not even have the option of experiencing obstacles. They don't exist anymore.

(LS) I'm guessing there won't be a line at the complaint department. Can you imagine? "Hey, I was shorted three obstacles."

(My Soul) Very funny, but if you've had obstacles, you've needed them, and the only reason you needed them was so that you could figure out on your own that you never needed them.

(LS) And you expect people to believe this? You just said two different things in the same sentence. That was a complete contradiction.

(My Soul) Absolutely not true. You need your obstacles so that you can *remember* your way back to your heart, back to love, back to who you really are. When you live as who you really are, you get to see the truth about your obstacles.

(LS) What is the truth about our obstacles?

(My Soul) They are as real as your tooth fairy.

(LS) To you maybe, but I can assure you that they are very real to us.

(My Soul) Okay, let's start from the beginning. Do you understand why a heart never breaks? The non-physical part of your heart, I mean.

(LS) Of course. A heart never breaks because it already is what we think we can't have.

(My Soul) Beautiful! Perfect. If you know this so well, why do you insist on claiming something that's not real?

(LS) Obstacles are real to me, and I am not my heart.

(My Soul) Who do you think you are?

(LS) Hey, the anger management class doesn't start until next week.

(My Soul) I mean that seriously. Do you think you are your body?

(LS) I'm not really sure who I am while I'm here. I guess I'm part physical and part non-physical, right?

(My Soul) Everything is one, so in one sense you're right, but your body is a part of you that you try on, like a pair of shoes or a jacket. Your true essence is your heart and when you comprehend this, you will finally know that you encountered obstacles only so that you could discover on your own that you never needed them—or better yet, that they never existed.

(LS) I get it. I get it. It's all about becoming, or realization, right?

(My Soul) It is *becoming* to you, *realization* to us, and *authenticity* at the highest level. Nothing is more real than your heart.

(LS) We spoke about how to get close to our heart, that is, closer to love in terms of our realization. I know that this is a part of love that most didn't even know was love, but what about romantic love? What is love?

(My Soul) Love is the soul of God and His greatest gift to us, so that we may bless ourselves and the world by also giving it away.

(LS) Beautiful. I understand completely, however everyone wants to *receive* love.

(My Soul) And there is no better way to receive love than to give it away. This is where you all run into a problem.

(LS) I understand why some people don't want to give love unless they believe they will receive it back, and I know this is the wrong way to go about it. However, it really is not easy to understand. We are saying, in essence, that if you love without wanting anything in return, you will have everything you want, except *don't* want it. This is quite confusing, to say the least.

(My Soul) That's not what we've said, and what we've said has never been the problem.

(LS) Then what is the problem, and what are we all doing wrong? It's as if love is a rare, precious jewel and only a very few are lucky enough to find it.

(My Soul) The problem is not the scarcity of love. The problem is the *elusiveness of authenticity.*

(LS) Oh, I *love* that! I think I get it, but can you explain it further?

(My Soul) Sure. The promise of anything to come because you loved, or more accurately, the *hope* of anything to come because you loved renders love counterfeit. Statements like, "I love you as long as you really love me," can never even come close to love.

(LS) I agree with everything here until you got to *hope*. How can it ever be bad to hope that you get what you want?

(My Soul) There is nothing wrong with hope in absolute terms, as long as you eventually move to belief, faith, and ultimately, to knowing. However, relative to what we give while loving someone, we start walking a thin line. We start hoping that something we do will make this person we love so much see that they love us, as well. We all have hoped that the one we love will love us, but love is more than that. Love *knows* everything is perfect. True love is an achievement that goes beyond hope. Few know better than you how difficult it is to be truthful with ourselves. I'm *not* saying that it's wrong to want to be loved by the one you love; I'm just asking you to be aware enough to separate what you want from what you give.

(LS) You say that as if it's the easiest thing in the world and all it takes is being aware.

(My Soul) I know it takes time and discipline, but awareness must come first. When you start to look at love and all of life from the perspective of why you're here, things will start to make sense to you that never did before.

(LS) Are you talking about love being the ultimate path to realization?

(My Soul) Love, along with all of life, but yes, love is your ultimate path, always.

(LS) The first thing we think of when the subject of love comes up is the way we will feel when we are loved as we have always wanted to be. I was certainly no exception to this, but my new awareness has made me understand that it is not only impossible to lose in love, but it is impossible to lose in any part of life.

(My Soul) Are we switching roles here? Am I now supposed to say, "No one will believe this," as you would have?

(LS) I know and understand why people will say this is crazy. I was one of them. But it's not crazy, and I'm hoping I can find a way to help my readers see the truth in this. The truth is beautiful.

(My Soul) Yes, love is even more beautiful than anyone has ever imagined, and you are well on your way to communicating this majestic truth to the world.

Love is an achievement, and everyone is on their way to it. Everyone is in the most perfect place for them right now, and no matter what happens, it will always inevitably lead to a higher level of love, just as yours has for you.

(LS) The hardest thing for me was separating what I wanted from my love. I suspect this is difficult for everyone. Once we understand that we must separate our love from what we want to receive in order for love to truly be authentic, guilt creeps in—at least it has for me. "Am I really worthy of what I want, and is it really okay to have my own desires?" Of course, I know that we are entitled to our desires, but in the beginning, it was hard for me to determine whether I was loving or just trying to get something. It takes a lot of coordination to love authentically while still having our personal desires and keeping them both separate.

(My Soul) Not only are you entitled to your desires, but they are your greatest opportunity for realization. At the same time, they teach those you love by example what's important and why we're here. Realization is the reason we're here, and love of all kinds is our most valued path to realization.

Pursuing what you love is also your greatest opportunity to serve God by expanding His/our universe. You would call it *His* universe and He would call it *ours*.

Expanding the universe benefits everyone, while giving financial support as an unearned gift usually hurts everyone. The person giving has less; the person receiving ends up with less no matter how much is given; and the entire universe is cheated out of its expansion. Almost your entire planet honors those who give in this way without knowing that it hurts literally everyone. This includes you, although to a lesser degree, now. There are some exceptions, like helping someone achieve a mission, a cause, or a purpose and as long as the support given doesn't become a dependency, or a moral hazard.

(LS) I thought we were supposed to be talking about love.

(My Soul) Did I strike a chord? Am I embarrassing you? What are you worried about? No one even knows that you spent your entire life as Robin Hood, minus the archery skills, of course.

(LS) Gee, thanks.

(My Soul) You want everyone to know the truth about you, right?

(LS) Yes, but is there a lesson in here somewhere, or are you just trying to torture me?

(My Soul) There's a lot more than just a lesson here. Can you really tell me that you don't know what good has already come out of what you've done?

(LS) I know it's good because I trust what has already happened, but it's really hard for me to see this one. All I honestly see is years of wasted time and money, and maybe decades would be more accurate. And where has all of this gotten me?

(My Soul) Was it supposed to get you somewhere? Were you expecting a return on your "investment?" Did you do it all for you?

(LS) I felt like I was helping people and myself at the same time. I really thought everyone was winning. I wanted everyone to win.

(My Soul) You wanted us to get back to talking about love because what you have done is embarrassing, and where you are today because of this and much more is even more embarrassing—and yet we *are* talking about love. We are talking about someone who has the courage to tell the truth about himself, no matter what the world might think. I know you thought I was berating you and giving you a beating, but on the contrary, I'm singing your praise.

(LS) You're singing my praise? I'm not sure where you learned how to sing, but I know it wasn't Juilliard.

(My Soul) This is not a slap in the face, and I am not trying to embarrass you. What you're doing is not easy. Taking a close look at yourself and finding the truths that you never wanted to face and admitting them to yourself—it's all a remarkable first step.

(LS) We were supposed to be talking about romantic love, so what does authenticity have to do with...ah...okay; now I get it.

(My Soul) Ah—beautiful. Please let me know when we need to change the light bulbs in your head; I want to make sure not to miss you when you've got that glow.

(LS) Okay, wise guy.

This is liberating, and it feels good, at least it does right now. I may reassess when I'm on the bread-and-water meal plan. Going through this process with you has not only made me more aware of myself, but more aware of others, as well. I'm more aware of how I and others are trying to feel and how we want to be seen by what we say and do. My awareness alone has helped me in a huge way here, and I'm hoping this book will help others. Even so, admitting even if only to ourselves that there is more to what we say and do than how it is seen is probably the most difficult thing I've ever done in my life. Here, I'm talking about the *reasons* we say what we say and the *reasons* we do what we do and being completely honest with ourselves about what those reasons are.

I was hiding behind the mask of generosity so that I could be seen the way I wanted to be seen and treated the way I wanted to be treated. I admit, I'm still generous, but I'm well aware of what I'm doing now and it's not all completely authentic all the time, but I'm getting much better. I want to take care of and protect the people I love the most without hurting them and I know how difficult this balance is. The same action done for completely different reasons has a completely different meaning and result, the difficult part is being honest with ourselves and I'm not completely where I want to be yet, but much better than I ever was.

This has gotten me into a lot of trouble. I would go to restaurants and tip an obscene amount. I thought this was the greatest thing, you know, "Everyone is happy, and all my *generosity* will come back to me a million times. I will continue to be rewarded for what I am doing for so many *other* people."

It wasn't all for them. It was for me. I have to tell you: the only time we will be rewarded is when we truly don't want to be. When all of the pleasure you get from giving is knowing that someone will now be okay, that is authentic love. That is truly caring, and ironically, I fell in love with someone who loved this way while I was writing this book.

(My Soul) Ironically? You know that every part of that relationship was planned, and you know the reasons why.

What I love most about what you just said was what *did not* come after; you never tried to defend who you are. Just beautiful. This will get people thinking about why they say what they say and why they do what they do, and it will inspire them to want to dive into this much more deeply.

(LS) Yes, it might also get me killed.

(My Soul) Don't you mean it could get you to heaven?

(LS) Look, I would love to go at the right time; I'm just kind of not finished here, yet.

(My Soul) Your turn. You will have to explain what this means to those who are not with us right now, and it will be therapeutic coming from you, as well.

(LS) I think you secretly love torturing me, but okay, here goes.

When we think of love as how much we desire someone who

does not desire us, we say that love hurt us, but the desire to get someone to want us who does not want us, can never be called love. Love is ours to give, and it is only ours to receive when all we want is to give it.

To do what you know is right for the one you love without needing to receive anything because of it is the highest form of love. Rejecting authentic love would be like trying to reject your soul: it can't be done. Your soul's only agenda is your enlightenment, and when you get your soul's messages, you're moving in the right direction. When you don't get your soul's messages, you are also moving in the right direction. You choose the road, and all roads lead to a higher version of your personality. You cannot make a mistake, and you cannot get lost. You can only take a different road to the same place. There is no wrong direction and there are no wrong choices. Every choice you make will ultimately lead to love and a higher version of you, even if you *choose* to go through fear, anger, frustration, and resentment to get there. There is no frustration on the part of your soul. Your soul is intimately aware that every choice you make is the right choice for you at that exact time.

There is a complicated formula that will always let you know if you made the right decision or took the right road for you. That formula is this—okay, get ready to write this down:

If you made the choice or *took the road,* it is the right one.

Now, you may say, "Yes, but I got hurt, or "Yes, but I hurt so many people."

I don't want to hurt people and I don't want anyone else to hurt people, certainly not intentionally. All I'm saying is that, if it happened, it happened to help you and everyone else became more as a result. Everyone becomes more, even when they are angry and not listening to the messages of feeling. Everyone becomes more, even when they are sure that nothing good has come out of what has happened. This is true because it is part of the process, part of the inevitable understanding and journey to enlightenment. This is why our hearts and souls are so valuable; they are delivering messages from God and all of His creations, from the Universe, Source Energy, Infinite Intelligence, and whatever else you want to call God's matrix.

Although love is the ultimate direction, even when a person chooses fear, it is also right. However, it is only right *after* it has been chosen, because fear is the path to love that they have chosen, and they can never *not* get there. They have just *decided*, for some reason, to shake and shiver their way to love. We have all chosen the path of fear at one time or another, although we didn't know it was a choice. Instead, we erroneously believed we didn't have a choice. So, when I say, that when you choose it, fear is right, I mean that it can only be right after you have already made the choice. The only reason it can be right is so that you can, on your own, decide *not* to choose fear at some point. My soul and I have said this many times: everything that happens, happens so that you can realize who you already are. You would understand this to mean *grow*, and if fear is something you chose, that was the best way for you to *realize*.

Our ideas of love are so deeply ingrained that it's difficult for us to see that there is much more to love than we have ever thought possible. Our original beliefs about love prevent us from seeing a higher truth.

This next quote is an example of love, right until the end, where he gets disconnected from love. Love never hurts. I know that many don't believe this is even possible, but when we all learn more about what love *really* is, we will *all* get this.

Loving you was a beautiful work of art. Although I never touched a brush, you got me to paint with my heart, sketching a world that neither of us ever saw; but it never really mattered, because somehow our hearts learned to draw. It's like when writers sit in quiet and write the words that we do to find that we never did the writing, because the words started writing you. The only way to be hurt in a love this true is to know that they're not happy when there's nothing we can do. —*Love Story*

This is the part of love that I still have a problem with. Love is trust, belief, faith, knowing, and understanding at the highest level. There can never be pain in knowing and understanding that everything that has already happened is absolutely the best thing that could have happened in terms of our growth and realization. When we can't see how this could be true, this is when we need love the most; this is when we need our belief, faith, knowing, understanding, and trust the most. When we hurt even because someone else is in a painful place, this doesn't mean we don't love them at the highest level we can. It just means that our moments of pain are not due to love.

Perhaps the situation most difficult for us to understand is watching a loved one suffer daily with terminal illness. How could anyone love such a person and not hurt for them? We all would think that anything other than hurting for them would be not caring. I completely understand, because I still do, as well. This takes a faith and trust beyond what I have been able to achieve.

I have a problem with it because I understand it intellectually, but not yet emotionally.

(My Soul) The personal story about your path from pretense to authenticity fits in well with your soliloquy on love. Kudos. You are all on an adventure to authenticity, but not everyone knows it, yet.

YOUR AUTHENTIC DESIRES
DIRECT YOU HIGHER

(My Soul) What you just wrote will help many people become more aware. Some will start to regret buying that car they loved so much before they bought it. What they didn't understand when they drove it out of the showroom was, the car owns them. The car tells them what they have to do every month in order to pay for it. Going after everything you want is your path to our purpose for you, so we want you to go after that car *if that is truly what you desire,* and we want you to go after it with everything you have.

We need your authentic desires to redirect you higher. Reaching for more enlightened desires that are not authentically yours because you have been advised to do so will always be a longer path to an authentic life. However, if this has already happened, the longer path is best for you, at least for the time you're on it.

There is not enough energy or power behind desires that are not truly yours, yet, for us to redirect you higher.

Eventually you will find out that the only reason you want anything material is so you can realize on your own that you don't really want it.

(LS) I think I started to arrive at that place when I wanted to rip the emblem off the hood of my car. I'm not there completely yet, but I definitely understand it.

(My Soul) Let's get back to your feeling guilty about feeling "good" when someone is suffering. I never said you have to feel good, but you will eventually get to a place where you know something good is coming from their suffering. This doesn't mean we don't have compassion, help them feel better, and love them as much as we can. It just means that we trust God's plan, and this is what faith is all about.

Real faith is trusting what we can't see or understand.

Think of the you who now knows this watching the you who got beaten up at school for six years.

(LS) I can't be sure I would make the right decision again. Even knowing that the result of it was a really good one—in fact, a beautiful one—I'm still not sure I could just watch it go on for so long without doing anything.

(My Soul) Don't forget, whatever you might have done would have been perfect for everyone. The fact is that no one stopped it until you did, and that was perfect for you and everyone else, whether they see that or not.

WHAT IS THE BEST WAY TO FIND LOVE?

(LS) WHAT IS the best way to find love? I think everyone would really want to know what we're supposed to do to find our soulmate.

(My Soul) Start from purpose. The purpose of love is to make you more, so go directly to making yourself more, first.

The very best way to find your soulmate is to do everything you can to *not* have it happen so that you will have time to work on becoming a better you in every area of your life. Create a personal life boot camp and commit to self-improvement in the areas of your life most important to you. *Do not* do this to be with someone or even to prepare to be with someone. Do it because this is what you want for you. Do not ask anyone else what you should be doing; only you can know what that is. Only you can connect to your heart in a way that knows what is most important to you. Find your own unique way to love yourself and the world, and when you do this, you will never have to search for love. Love will search for you.

We already are and already have everything we have ever wanted, but we just have not *realized* it yet. Realization is both the awareness that we already have what we want and the act of displaying that reality because we know that it's true. Working on you is a path of love, as well as a path to realization. Create your own personal boot camp and design it to improve the most important aspects of your life from your perspective. Work on *becoming* the ideal you. You may at first think this has nothing to do with love and attempt to dismiss it, so allow me to explain why it is so important. Not only are you loving yourself, but this is a powerful way to go directly to the result of love, first.

Love is a gift designed to make you more, in *your* terms, and to help you to realize who you have always been in *ours*, so go directly to making yourself more now, because regardless of what you think, no one falls in love with the way you look, and no one ever has. People fall in love with *who* you are.

The way you look attracts people to you, but it does not cause them to fall in love with you.

If the objective is to find love, *don't* try to find it. Your love can only be real when it is not an attempt to receive *anything* in return, including, of course, to be loved in return. No one should ever want to be loved *in return*. Instead, you should *choose* to be loved. Love *in return* is like a favor, done only through reciprocation, and it can't possibly be authentic. Wanting something that is not at the level of *choosing* is not yet touching love. *Choosing* is an achievement, which means you have reached a level of *knowing* that you can make a selection. *Choosing* is in contrast to *wanting* something you don't yet *know* that you can have, or *choose*.

(LS) And *choosing* to be loved is what we talked about when we were discussing prayer and affirmations, right?

(My Soul) Yes, you create being loved, using the tools you've been given. And because love is the highest level of faith, *wanting* something that is not at the level of *choosing* is not yet love.

(LS) I really do understand that, now, but it sounds like you're making love an impossible achievement. Are you saying that most of the world doesn't yet love? Because people are not going to be okay with that.

(My Soul) I'm not interested in what most people will be

okay with. Only you are. But it sounds like you will be pleased to know that everyone loves, but not everyone is aware that they do—speaking of love from my perspective, of course.

Every one of you loves at the highest level, because contrary to your beliefs, no heart has any desires. A heart has only realities, which means that your heart is always living *above* the levels of faith and knowing.

(LS) Okay, so when we say we love someone, we do, but possibly only in a way we're not yet aware of.

(My Soul) Exactly. Your heart is always loving, whether you're aware of it or not. Only the parts of you that are not connected to me or your heart get disappointed, discouraged, anxious, and fearful.

(LS) But if you are a part of me, aren't we always connected?

(My Soul) Ah, what a perfect question to ask. Of course, we are, always, but your belief—or I should say disbelief—makes your life and world appear disconnected from me. You paint your world in the color of your beliefs. Many in your world go through life trying to make all the right connections. "It's not what you know, but who you know," they've been told, while neglecting the most important and most valuable connection. You have been one of these people, but that is all changing for you now.

(LS) Can you tell me how that's changing for me? I'm not quite sure what you mean by that.

(My Soul) Your ideas and decisions are starting to flow through our mission for you. This is not yet true in every situation in your life, but it is a major difference from the decisions you've made in the past.

(LS) Are you talking about choosing love?

(My Soul) When you need something to happen and it is the most important thing in your life—a desperate situation like the reason this book came to life—you usually do not choose love. But this time, you did, and I'm happy to see it continuing. Choosing love always serves both you and me, even when it is not yet apparent that our missions are linked. Even choosing pretense is just a longer path to love.

(LS) Oh, my God! This conversation is going quite a bit beyond what I ever could have imagined. Thank you.

(My Soul) I would hope that's a good thing.

(LS) It is. I just worry about losing people, here. This conversation is not only for me, now.

(My Soul) Stop being concerned about what you already know. You know the value of this conversation, and you also know that there are parts of it that not everyone will be ready for. Truly loving them would be allowing them to be who they are and allowing their own realization to unfold at their own perfect pace. Your insistence on the *need* for things to be the way you want them to be is what keeps what you want away from you. Do you see this?

(LS) Yes, thank you! Can we get back to how working on ourselves will attract our soulmate?

(My Soul) Please.

(LS) I honestly don't think people are going to believe that, if we just work on ourselves, the love of our life will fall from the sky.

(My Soul) Thankfully.

No one has ever fallen in love with someone because of the way they look, and no one ever will. Now looks may have been the initial attraction that caused you to connect in the first place, but it is never the reason we fall in love. We fall in love with who people *are*, not with how they look. This is kind of like when you pick up a book because you love how the cover looks, but if you fall in love with it, it's only because you love what's inside.

Every one of you was great before you were born, and you didn't lose anything when you got here. Every one of you is a genius. Don't you see what you have been doing? You have been judging a cat on its ability to bark, and then agreeing with your world that you are a failure. You are *different* than they are, and yet they insist on judging you as if you *are them*.

I don't care who you are or what you have done; you have been brought here to love your life and be authentically you, and if you feel like a failure, it's only because you are trying to be *them*, and if not *them*, who *they* want you to be. You are so beautifully different from even those you respect and admire. Every one of you is beautiful, and every one of you has the ability to affect the world in your own way. Love yourself enough to know that you are not supposed to be anyone but *you*. A fisherman never takes his boat out for hours only to feel disappointed that he has not shot even one deer.

(LS) So, I should never have been disappointed that I was not a Michael Jordan or a Jerry West. And in bringing up Jerry West, I'm definitely dating myself—which is what I do when no one else will.

(My Soul) It's been a while since you broke into comedic Tourette's. We still have a lot to do.

(LS) Deal.

(My Soul) Of course, you should not be disappointed that you are not like someone else. You have found who you are, and don't be surprised when who you are changes, even if slightly.

(LS) So, I have found my purpose?

(My Soul) Good to see that you are still playing the role of the reader.

You have found your *path* to your purpose.

Your unique path to your purpose is hidden in your heart, and it's your soul's unparalleled, artfully choreographed use of pain and pleasure that will eventually prompt you to decide, on your own, to join your heart.

You don't get to choose your purpose, but you do choose

how you get there. The path to our purpose always runs through your heart; we cannot get to purpose any other way. Those who say they have given up all that is in their heart to go directly to enlightenment instead, if in fact they follow through on this, are not yet aware that enlightenment has become the largest part of their heart.

You choose your path to our purpose.

From your perspective, you choose what you feel is your purpose or mission in life, but this is not your ultimate purpose or mission. What you call your purpose is what we call your path to our higher purpose. From your perspective, we are infinitely more evolved than you are; but from our perspective, you are us, and so, you are just as evolved as you believe we are, only you can't see that yet. Does this make sense to you now?

Your heart and I play distinctly different roles while this masterful collaboration shares the same purpose, and we wait patiently for the day that you join us.

(LS) Didn't you just say that I was you?

(My Soul) You are, but that doesn't mean you have joined us. You still live most of your life as if you are not.

(LS) Where am I in this process?

(My Soul) You are starting to join us, and we can tell by how you now react and respond to disappointment. You trust us more than most do, and so your family and friends don't understand how you do not hurt more than they think you should under certain circumstances.

(LS) I do hurt, still.

(My Soul) Yes, and you still will, but it's starting to change. Some people who care about you think you no longer care about them, but they have no way of knowing about your evolution.

(LS) Wait—I'm not sure I want this evolution. In many ways, I care even more than I used to, and I certainly do hurt.

(My Soul) Evolution is not your choice; it merely unfolds.

You do care more, and you do hurt, of course, but you don't *need* or require approval in the same way you did. Your caring is more real, now. Yes, you get confused and thrown off, but you have grown so much even in the last few weeks. You have been through a lot in the last few months, and you have handled it well.

(LS) Not everyone will agree with that.

(My Soul) What matters is what you agree with. Understand why you have taken the criticism you have taken. Think about how you would have handled this situation even a year ago.

(LS) I never thought of that, but I would have completely fallen apart, and actually, I did initially.

(My Soul) Your image is not as wrapped up in what others think as it used to be. Now, today, you are still dealing with probably the most difficult thing you've ever dealt with, and you still fear how this will be taken. You still fear the response of many people, so you are not out of the woods by any stretch, but you have made huge progress, and many great things are to come.

(LS) Thank you for seeing me through all this.

(My Soul) What else would I do? I have always been here for you. I am always here for *everyone*. It was you who found me, and now you can help everyone find me; and in so doing, they will be finding themselves.

(LS) I can't wait.

(My Soul) It's coming. There is a lot more coming, and I see you are getting ready. So good to see you listening to us.

(LS) Of course—but what does this have to do with our purpose?

(My Soul) You can only get to our purpose for you by going through your heart, and you will need to not be influenced by what others think of you in order to do that. Who would know this better than you? You hear about it every day, and you live it every day. Your journey has been specifically designed for you to realize this. Everyone's journey has been custom designed to take a different path to the same place, a path for their realization only. You were all part of the design team, and not only for *your* journey.

(LS) Can you tell me whose journey I am a part of?

(My Soul) Absolutely. You are just now starting to be aware of how others affect your journey without knowing that they're doing so. Everyone and everything has a journey, and you are all an intricate part of every journey.

(LS) I'm really starting to understand this. It is astounding. Our heart is like a road map to your mission for us.

(My Soul) Exactly.

(LS) In many ways, we actually are honored by being pulled away from our hearts and called selfish and much worse just for staying loyal to our hearts.

(My Soul) Your heart is God's plan for you. It can never be forsaken. This does *not* mean that you abandon your friends or family. The understanding that you don't have to give up one for the other is a level of faith that many of you have not yet reached.

I love you so much that I will *never* give up my dreams for you, but will go to the end of the earth and back to make sure you never give up on yours.

This is my vow to you, and it should be yours to everyone you love. This is how you should love your world, including your close friends and family, of course. It is so much easier to make them happy than to do the right thing, and even more so when they are honoring you for choosing them over your heart. However, they don't yet know that what they see as you choosing your heart over them is actually choosing *them* in the most glorious way. They may not follow you initially, because they won't always see what you're doing as right. Maybe also they see you as a failure, but if this occurs it is good for them and you, and you must trust it. Eventually, we get to them, at the time that is perfect for everyone's journey.

(LS) Yes, I agree, and I completely understand, but people do get pulled away from their hearts. I can see why. I have friends and relatives with whom I have no connection or contact, anymore. I used to be very close to all of these people. Am I really supposed to just let go forever?

(My Soul) That is not even possible.

(LS) What is not possible?

(My Soul) You can focus in another direction, but you cannot get rid of any part of you for any period of time, and it is not possible *not* to have contact. The more you say someone has no influence on you, the more they do. Do you see more clearly how valuable your best friend has been to you, now?

(LS) Best friend?

(My Soul) You know who I'm talking about.

(LS) I have always seen her as valuable.

(My Soul) Come on now. If you're being honest, you know that's not true.

(LS) Yes, there are times I have not seen her as valuable to me; that's true. I felt captured by negative emotion and didn't even think to try to understand, at least in the very beginning.

(My Soul) Without exception, everything is *for* us; so the next time you're hurt, think about that. I know you know this and you get it right most of the time, but there are no exceptions, remember that.

(LS) I will, thank you so much.

The situation with my friend was not easy for me because of how much of my identity is a direct result of all she has done for me—from where I live and how I live, to the friends I have and even to what I read, to some degree. I would probably not have a car if it hadn't been for her—her and her husband, actually. There is so much more. Probably an entire book could be written on this situation, but it won't be. They are all really good people and are beyond amazing parents. We had a pure friendship, pure in the sense that all we wanted from each other was the opportunity to help each other, nothing else, until that changed.

What a beautiful way it was to live. It was a perfect friendship, and she was more like my family than a friend. Ultimately, we changed from two people who brought out the best in each other to two people who brought out the worst in each other. It got to the point that it was no longer healthy for us to even speak to each other or communicate in any way. At first, it confused me and was even painful, but it's not anymore. I honestly believe I truly understand the purpose behind our friendship for the period of time we had it, as well as why we don't speak today. I really trust you, and so I don't question if this is good for everyone. But why does so much of my life have to be painful? Does it always have to be like this?

(My Soul) You have chosen pain. I did not, and it doesn't have to be like this. You had plenty of choices, and you still do. You want to know why things are the way they are, and it doesn't benefit you to know all of it right now.

(LS) Okay, I trust you. I can't say I like it very much, but I trust you.

(My Soul) Trusting is more important than liking.

(LS) Ugh.

(My Soul) To stay on your path and be true to your heart is not always easy. It takes knowing who you are and being true to yourself, and everything that has happened is helping you reach that. Those you love and who love you will test your faith, as well, and mostly without the awareness that they are doing so.

Your world sees it as beautiful to give up what you love for whom you love, and this is your greatest illusion. Giving up what you love can *never* be good for who you love.

(LS) I know without any doubt, now, that this is true, but it's so hard to do. It is so hard to make decisions knowing that those you love will *believe* that because of those decisions, you no longer love them as much as you once did. Even worse, at times they question how much you ever did love them. I would never chose approval over love because of what I know to be true. I wouldn't be able to live with myself. I used to, but would never do it again.

(My Soul) Wouldn't you feel good about giving up what you love for whom you love? Your entire world honors and celebrates all who make such sacrifices.

(LS) No, and it's the opposite. Knowing that possibly the entire world has different beliefs than I do makes it even harder for me to do what I know serves us all, but I do hope this book helps people understand.

(My Soul) Do you not see this as arrogant? Are you saying that you know something the entire world doesn't?

(LS) Of course not. It is impossible for me to know something that others do not know. Every one of us is the entire world and the entire universe; we just are not *consciously* aware that we are. I learned this from you, and you are a part of everyone, so they already know—only they don't know that they know, yet.

(My Soul) So beautiful. To see what this has done for your awareness is what I live for, and by "your," I mean everyone and everything.

(LS) Yes, I know it can be no other way. Thank you, and I could not do it without you.

(My Soul) It is not possible for you to do anything without me, for even when you are not *allowing* me, through your words and actions, I am still here. These are always the times when you question God and why things happen to you and those you love.

(LS) Yes, I know this very well. Things that happen crush many people. I know, because they have crushed me in the past, and I understand why people get frustrated and overwhelmed by all that happens *to* them. When there is too much to handle, many people see life as being unfair and even at times think that God is against them. Too many just give up, because they can't see even a hint of evidence to support continuing.

(My Soul) The evidence is everywhere you turn.

(LS) I know this, now, but how can you expect people to see that from where they are? I know exactly how they feel; I have been just as lost.

(My Soul) You think I should make it easier for everyone?

(LS) I'm not saying to hand it to us, but make it easier to grow from, make it easier to uncover and understand. At times, we get so demoralized we want to give up, and many of us do, so how can that be helping us?

(My Soul) Would you rather be less valuable than you are? Would you rather everyone be less valuable? You are asking to become a watered-down version of who you are. Ultimately, you are asking to be less and for everyone else to be less, too. We will never rob you of your true identity and the character you build by going through everything you do to get to realization. Anything we *give* you, in your terms, will be *taken from* you in ours.

(LS) Wow! I never thought of it that way. Thank you! So, does this mean that the more we are given, the less we become?

(My Soul) Well, it's all up to you, and it doesn't have to be this way, but the more you are given, the more your chances of *realization* diminish.

(LS) Why is that?

(My Soul) The more you're given, the less you will do, and the less you have to figure out on your own, generally.

(LS) So glad you added the word *generally* in there, because I have been given a ton. My life could have been so easy, so comfortable, so peaceful, but instead I have created more problems and more pain than anyone could imagine. And yet, I love my life more now than ever. Okay, so what's wrong with me?

(My Soul) The discovery that your life is an adventure to authenticity has changed everything for you. You see the world differently. You understand more about what your so-called failures really mean. I use the word *failures* from your perspective only, because we know that there are none.

(LS) Wait—let's talk about that, because it looks like *everything* in my life has been a failure. My readers somehow see me differently. When I write about some particular failure in my life, they say, "But look at you, now!" Many people see me as successful, and the truth is that I have been a failure at everything; not from your perspective, I know, but at least in the way most people would see it, using the traditional definition of success. The real truth is that I have had some fleeting success in some things, and at times, some appear pretty miraculous, but in the end, it all fell apart.

(My Soul) The difference between you and us is that we see the truth, not just something you made up because you don't like the results.

(LS) You're being just a little harsh, don't you think?

(My Soul) It's exactly what you do; you all do it. What you call failure is nothing more than us redirecting you to a better place, but instead of going to the better place, you take it personally.

(LS) It seems to be my experience that whenever I

experience a really huge "failure" in something, it is the end of that particular part of my life, and a new life is being born.

(My Soul) It is certainly no failure; it is more like your graduation present.

(LS) Maybe you should stay home at my next graduation.

(My Soul) You are my home.

(LS) You know I was kidding, right?

(My Soul) How can I not? By the way, except for using the word "failure," you put it perfectly.

Whenever you're in any kind of pain, think of a mother giving birth and understand that your pain also means that some beautiful miracle is trying to be born.

(LS) Beautiful. Thank you so much. I know that's true now, and I knew it was before I realized that I was talking to you.

I was so good at portraying an artificial image that many people saw me as very successful. I did have temporary success in certain areas, but it was not even close to what I portrayed. I made people believe I was something I was not—and I didn't know I was doing this because I even believed it myself. I never once thought to myself that I was living a lie. I don't think of this as sad; in fact, I love it that everything happened exactly as it did. I can honestly say that I have not even one regret in my life.

Everything that has ever happened to you and everything you have ever done makes up the masterpiece called you. "No regrets" does not mean you want to do those things again. "No regrets" means...

I love who I am.

Be grateful for everything; thank God for everything.

~~Love Story~~

This is *exactly* how I feel. I really *love* who I am, and I am beyond grateful for *everything*. I know it may be hard for some people to believe, especially those who know some of what I've been through, but there is absolutely *nothing* that I wish never happened; and of course, there's nothing I wish I'd never done, as well. I don't like hurting people, and I would love it if there were a different way for me to get where you're taking me, but I trust you completely.

I have a serious challenge ahead of me, and I am happy that I do. I really understand who you are to me, and I love our collaboration.

(My Soul) Now, that was incredible. It is so beautiful to watch the evolution of your realization. You have a long road ahead of you, but it is very inspiring to watch you uncover who you are.

(LS) I inspire *you*?

(My Soul) Absolutely, and you always have. You all inspire me. Telling me how "great" you are, when coming from you, is really telling me where you are not, yet. And you are great, but not in the way you have described yourself in the past. Telling me who you really are—now that is inspirational. Your adventure to authenticity is going well.

(LS) What about those like me, or like who I used to be, who try to be seen the way we want to be seen? Do we inspire you? How could I inspire you when I was so pathetic?

(My Soul) Every one of you inspires me all the time. You see, you forget that I know who you really are, even when you have forgotten. I know what you have coming. Where you are doesn't matter; but what I really mean is, where you *think* you are doesn't matter. Who you are is what matters, and who you are is never in dispute, not from us.

You are saying a lot of things about yourself here that you have never said before. Aren't you worried about opening yourself up to being attacked by those who would love to hurt you? And that those who love you and really care about you may believe those attacks? Aren't you afraid of losing support?

(LS) Have we switched roles here?

(My Soul) I think it would be good to show where you are at this point; so yes, temporarily.

(LS) What can someone possibly say about me that I haven't already?

I would much rather lose support for being real than gain support for being fake.

(My Soul) I love that!

(LS) You gave it to me.

(My Soul) But you said you have this big thing you need to take care of—aren't you worried that you will not sell enough books if you make yourself look like such a horrible person?

(LS) The reason I'm writing the truth is because that's exactly the way it is, and I have learned to love the way it is. What I choose to take care of is already done; it's just that the time delay has not yet caught up. It is created and being lived every day, so nothing else can possibly happen. Not to mention that pretending has made me neither happy nor wealthy.

(My Soul) I can feel how you feel when you communicate this. It is so much more real to you now than it ever was. And pretending was not all bad, as it was the path you took to where you are today. Because it has unfolded this way, there could have been no better path for *you* at that specific time.

(LS) Really? You can feel that? Thank you. It feels so great to be where I am.

(My Soul) Of course I can. Did you forget who I am?

(LS) No, but I have said similar words many times before, and then I start working on something physically: making calls, meeting people, getting rejected, and being criticized, and old doubts start to creep in.

(My Soul) Don't you understand that no matter who you are talking to, they can't possibly know more about what we're talking about than you do now? I'm not saying you're smarter than anyone else. I'm just saying that this is yours. You gave birth to this. This is your offspring, and no DNA test is required.

(LS) Is that really true? I mean, there are many parts to *our* philosophy that I have never witnessed anyone communicate in any form prior to now, but there are also many people whom none of us ever hear from who dedicate their entire lives to their philosophy. There are many from indigenous tribes, like Tibetan monks, who don't write books or go on talk shows. They are far beyond people like me.

(My Soul) They are beyond you in their own way, and they live what they say more accurately than you do at this point, but your philosophy is yours and their philosophy is theirs, and there is no need to measure.

(LS) Then how does everyone know which one is right?

(My Soul) Their philosophy is perfect for their journey, just as your philosophy could not be any better for yours. And in anticipation of your next question, readers will pick up exactly what will enhance their journey at the time they read it. All of this will serve them well when they—what?

(LS) Listen to feeling!

TRAGEDY AND FAILURE; MY GREATEST BLESSINGS EVER

(MY SOUL) KUDOS. Okay, I hope you don't mind if I change the subject here for a minute, because I think this is very important.

(LS) Jesus, take the wheel.

(My Soul) Ah, it is beautiful when you show how much you know who I am. Only now, if you could muster the strength to never take it back and let me keep it forever, that would really be *you* keeping it. Do you understand this? Do you understand how beautiful this *will be*?

(LS) Wow! That was so amazing I had to read it over several times. I really do understand, and I've been working hard on letting go and allowing you.

(My Soul) Yes, that's exactly what I want to talk about. Throughout this conversation, I have criticized you for not committing at the level you will need to in order to *fix* what you used to say is broken.

(LS) Yes, so happy to see you put "used to" in there, and, yes, I'm going to take care of it. This is my most important mission, right now.

(My Soul) And now I'm happy to say that it truly shows. You have locked yourself in a hotel in Albuquerque, New Mexico. The only time you see people is when you go to Squeezed to get your six cold-pressed organic juices for the day. You've been getting up at four a.m. every morning, even when you go to bed after midnight. You work on this mission from four a.m. until you can't keep your eyes open anymore, and if you are not yet finished for the day when your eyes start closing, you rest for an hour or so, come back, and finish.

You have committed to giving up food for more than two months and replaced it with cold-pressed organic juice, flooding your body with juice that has just been made. You do this because you know that this is what will make you healthy and full of enough energy to accomplish this mission. I will really enjoy watching you continue this, as I now know you will.

(LS) Thank you so much. It feels great to commit at this level. I feel great; although today is day four of my 75-day juice fast, and the detox is making me feel a little sick, right now. But I know that most likely the nausea will be gone by tomorrow.

(My Soul) Don't you think it's time, yet?

(LS) Time?

(My Soul) We have talked about a lot here, and I know that getting to this place was not easy for you.

(LS) You mean to the truth?

(My Soul) Yes, the truth about most things, but not about everything. And all I'm saying is, isn't it time, now? I know not all of what happened and what you did is only your business, but you can tell what is your business. Also, maybe you can tell everyone the real reason behind your cold-pressed organic juice fasting and cleansing?

(LS) The answer is, yes. Now is the time. Let me start with the juice fasts.

This is easy to explain, because I didn't really know what was going on for a long time. I can't say for sure, even now, that I know everything I need to know about this, but I'll give it my best shot.

When I was about ten or eleven, my father told me that I was the most expensive part of his household budget. From as long as I can remember, I had an exceptionally large appetite. It was always this way, and for a really long time, I never gained any weight because, if I wasn't eating or sleeping, I was playing basketball, running hills, running around a track, and more. Honestly, even today, there is almost nothing I don't do to extremes, but I'm finding now, finally, that if I don't change some of these things, I will probably not be walking this planet for too much longer. I seriously believe that, and it actually helps that I do.

I know I need to make some permanent changes and that my life depends on it, now. I know it doesn't look at all like it's this urgent to my friends and family or anyone who knows me, but *I* know, and the only time I remember not wanting to eat massive amounts of food was after my first sixty-day, cold-pressed organic juice fast. I watched a documentary, *Fat Sick and Nearly Dead,* by Joe Cross. It's a good inspirational documentary.

The fast is an incredible thing to do. It's a chance to start all over, because you have to force yourself to want the same foods again. After the fast, it's impossible to eat anywhere near the amount you used to, even if you only ate normal-size meals before. This is coming from someone who has eaten forty pancakes, six eggs, and a pound of bacon for breakfast and was still only 170 pounds. But that was a long time ago. I was a teenager. I had to be crazy to think I could continue to eat like that without it affecting me.

Of course, I want to look good, but more than anything, this is about air. It's about being able to breathe. It's about loving myself. I had cleverly learned how to take breaths in between words so I wouldn't suffocate when I spoke, and only my kids seem to know when I was doing this. The diagnosis was always asthma and COPD, but no medication that was ever given to me worked, not even a little. I was hospitalized with pneumonia twice, once for almost a month, and when I didn't respond to the intravenous antibiotics, out of desperation, the doctors requested I take an AIDS test. It came back negative. No one knew what to do.

Months later, I said to my doctor, "I know what it is. I finally got it." I went on to explain what had happened after I had eaten a particularly large meal. He told me that my problem had nothing to do with food, but on my insistence, he gave me a complete food allergy test. This came back negative, also, but what they didn't know was that a normal daily dinner for me would be four double cheeseburgers, a large fries, and don't even ask about desert and about a gallon of water. I was killing myself, and I didn't want to admit it, not even to me.

So, when I saw Joe Cross's first documentary, I decided I would try the juice cleanse. I am an extremist in life, not in the customary political definition, but in my personal life, so if you tried to get me to stick to a conventional diet, it would probably never happen. But not eating for almost an entire summer—no problem.

(My Soul) Do you realize that you have never told anyone that story as completely as you just did now, right here?

(LS) Yes, I know this is the first time, but it's always easier to talk about something you did after you've fixed it. This is why it's so difficult to talk about my "other blessing." I know it's "fixed." I know now that it can be no other way, but those I've blessed in what I used to call my nightmare won't see this as a blessing to them, and I may not have enough credibility for them to believe me when I tell them the truth. Yet, I know I'm not supposed to make them believe it; they will discover the truth at the right time for them.

(My Soul) But aren't you at least a little afraid of how this will look?

(LS) Yes, I still am, and I know you know that. I'm not out of the woods, yet, but I know the truth, and I'm working on that realization every moment I can. What I used to call my worst failure ever has become my greatest blessing, and I don't just mean this book and this conversation, although they're so much more valuable than I could have ever dreamed. In, what I used to call my tragedy, I have the opportunity to turn every part of it into a blessing and not just for me and those directly involved, but for everyone. I have a friend who does not have that luxury. She can grow from what happened, she can achieve some type of realization, but she can't fix it. No matter what she does, she cannot bring her daughter back. My problem seems so small and insignificant when I think of what happened to my friend. I honestly believe that losing a child is the worst thing that anyone can go through.

(My Soul) Please understand that what happened *for* you was something we knew would get you to finally discover who you really are, it could not have been planned more perfectly. Life is always happening *for* you, but that doesn't mean you're going to like it. Your knowing of the truth has gotten progressively better and is now at unprecedented levels for you, but if your knowing was where we want it to be, there would be no fear, anywhere. Do you understand this?

(LS) Yes, I do, and thank you for reminding me of it.

(My Soul) I know that most of the time you don't worry about this at all, but there are certain triggers that can still pull you off until you work your way back. When those triggers no longer pull you off, even in a really small way, not only do you know that worry is completely gone, but what you want to see physically is about to be born.

Okay, get back to your other blessing, and we'll continue this later.

(LS) Wow! Thank you.

I was going to remain on my cold-pressed, organic juice fast for 75 days, but I stopped at 65 because I was working out too hard and too early and went into such calorie deficit that I got dizzy.

I can take a deep breath and completely fill my lungs for the first time, probably since I was a little kid. My joint pain and swelling are completely gone, which I honestly didn't think was possible since I'd had joint pain and swelling when I was in my teens. The only thing I can think of that might cause joint pain and swelling at thirteen years old is excess toxins from the massive amounts of food I ate daily, even when I was thirteen. I thought the swelling in my knees was completely gone when I did the fast for 60 days last time, but this time I'm at a new and better level. I have lost exactly 62 pounds in the 65 days, a loss of 98 pounds from my original high. I honestly feel better than I can ever remember.

People who don't need to get knee replacements are getting them, and I know this is true because I used to be in so much pain and was so swollen that I was unable to move normally. Today, I can run distances that I was unable to walk only two months ago, and with absolutely no pain. I know this sounds great, but this is the *least* valuable gift from the entire program I'm on, and it's more than just juice. For me, not having the joint pain is *huge*, because it's something I've lived with since I was a little kid. But so much more beneficial than the 98 pounds I lost and the end of joint pain has been the resolution of a lifelong breathing issue that no medicine had been able to help, not even a little. Today, it is gone, without leaving even the slightest trace that it had ever been there. If you have ever struggled to get air to keep yourself alive, or even just keep yourself conscious, you know what I'm talking about.

(My Soul) Such a beautiful way of loving yourself as well as a testament to what your bodies are capable of; and yet you have not even touched the surface in terms of explaining what this can do.

Okay, it's time to tell about what you did that caused this to be a conversation and ultimately a book. I know this is a little more difficult for you, because people won't see this as having been "fixed," yet, and although fewer and fewer, there are still some times when you don't.

(LS) Yes, yes, I know.

Many years before I was born, my uncle managed his father's finances, and he did a great job for a long time, but he made one mistake. So, he called his father and said that he needed to come to his house and talk to him face to face. Now, my uncle lived in

America, while his father lived in Italy, so his father knew it was something extremely serious. After a long trip, he finally made it into his father's living room. His father said, "What are you doing here? What is so important that you couldn't tell me on the phone?"

His son said, "We had a little problem in the stock market, and we've been wiped out." He was deathly afraid of what his father was going to do to him. His father, standing in his living room and looking into the eyes of his son, who just traveled across the globe to tell him something he knew was not easy for his son to do, said, "I did it once, I'll do it again, and I hope you learned your lesson, because you're going to continue managing my money, only you're going to do it right this time." At that moment, my uncle felt more respect for his father than he'd ever felt for anyone.

It's possible I have some details wrong, but this is the story that was told to me. I was very close to my aunt and uncle, but neither of them had ever told me this story, and now I understand why.

Well, his father did make all that money again, and my uncle clearly learned his lesson, as well, because the original money that my uncle's father had made went into a trust for the most important people in my life, along with separate money for me. And now, I have made the exact same mistake as my uncle, and I am on a daily mission to successfully complete what I was trusted to complete. What are the odds that the same money from the same person would be lost twice, and for the same reason, fifty to seventy-five years later?

The situation was killing me every day for almost a year, and even after I understood why it had happened, it was still extremely difficult to deal with. And when I talk about why this happened, I don't mean why I made the mistake; I mean the purpose of what I now call, "My greatest blessing ever."

TO YOU

CHOOSE A PATH OF LOVE

MANY TIMES IN my life I have disappointed people, only to be left devastated, because I never understood that I didn't have to place my value in the hearts, minds, and hands of those I love. Sometimes, we find ourselves in a place where those who once looked up to us no longer do. Maybe they no longer ask for advice as they once did, for example. When that's true, as painful as it may be, it is designed to be the perfect hammer and chisel for us at that moment.

I have been on both sides of this kind of disappointment many times in my life, however, this time is different for me. Instead of feeling devastated, or even worse in this situation, I'm actually excited. I get to see a truth that only someone who has spent much time alone, in silence, can possibly see. Today, I see my situation as my greatest opportunity, ever. What we do, or fail to do in our lives does not make us more or less valuable, and although I know this, I still find myself assessing the value of others and my value in this way, at times.

The "occurrence" of this book has made me see a truth I never could have seen without it. Self-made billionaires will be buried just as far under the same ground as you and I, and their life of success, as perceived by the world, does not make them more valuable than everyone else. Your life journey, including everything you did and didn't do, is by far your most valuable path to realization, and at the time and in the manner it all happened—period. There are no exceptions. This doesn't mean you don't care about what you do or about the people who don't understand you. The path to our purpose is paved in red, and we are meant to pursue the contents of our hearts, regardless of what anyone says or how we are judged for whom and what we love.

It's not just *okay* to pursue your authentic desires—you cannot complete your purpose for being here without doing so.

Your soul needs your authentic desires to redirect you to a higher place, and when you replace your own authentic desires with a supposedly more enlightened desire of someone other than you, you lack the energy your soul needs to redirect you higher.

My greatest blessing ever came disguised as my most epic failure, and the only thing that made that clear was my response to it. There have been times in my life when I responded with the same level of commitment as I did with this situation, and these are all my most treasured accomplishments. Although I have not yet accomplished what I am committed to as I write this, I have reached a place where I can feel my level of commitment moving the universe. If there is anything in this world that I am qualified to speak on, it is failure, for I have never met anyone who has failed as many times or on a larger scale than I have—I am speaking of failure as it is measured by the world's standards, of course. Although my definition of success has certainly changed over the years, there are certain areas of my life involving money that I choose to take care of at last.

I would much rather die broke and a complete failure by the world's standards, yet doing what I love to do and with a huge smile on my face, than to live an unhappy, miserable life while being seen as hugely successful at executing the dreams and obligations of those who couldn't tell you one thing about me.

When I speak about failure as my greatest blessing ever, I

mean this only *after* the failure has occurred. Any intention to produce tragedy or failure in an attempt to reap their blessings is a deliberate path to self-destruction, and that's not what I'm talking about, here. I seem to unconsciously have experience with this, as well, as so much of my life seems like an attempt to destroy myself.

Everyone wants to be proud of how they look, and everyone wants to live the lifestyle they desire, but your bank account and your physical appearance will always be the least accurate measures of your value.

Your value is not in what you give others or what you do for them; your true value is who you and others become as a result of how you made them feel.

This is the way it really is. I know that's not the way we want it to be, but we can all get what we want when we learn to align our dreams with our soul's mission for us. The way we do this is by choosing a path of love to get everywhere we want to go. And when we don't know where we want to go, an expression or display of love will find your path for you. When I encourage you to choose love to get where you want to go, I am not contradicting myself and adding a condition to love. Love can have no conditions or it must be called something else. Choosing love to get what you want does not mean using ultimatums. It means you are also choosing the highest level of faith.

Everyone has desires, and this is not just okay, for your unique heart is the road map to your journey only, and that has been given to you by God. Not only are we meant to use this road map, we are also meant to inspire everyone we love to use their road maps; and we all do, whether we know we are doing so or not. This book is an example. People have inspired me who would say they have not, but this is only because they are not yet aware that they have.

The story of how I became a writer (the path to my mission)

is a story about aligning my heart with my soul. I am, right now, working with my team on something that we plan to make our greatest-ever experience of love by aligning our desires with our souls' mission for us—and not just as an example—but because we truly believe in it. I talk here about one example after another in my life, as if my life has always been a shining example of what I write, and nothing can be further from the truth. I just want you to see what's possible when we align our desires with our soul's mission for us.

I know it's not easy to believe that everything serves our greater purpose and that everything is *for* us and never *against* us, so I want to tell you a personal story. I know without a doubt that no one walking the planet at the time this occurred would have been able to see anything positive coming —not for me or for anyone.

From grade school to my first year in high school, I was beaten, sometimes pretty badly. I was bullied three to four times a week for about six years during the school year, and although much less often, it continued during the summer. Wiping the blood off my face before going in my house after school became as commonplace as washing my hands after dinner. I experienced a lot of physical pain, although the embarrassment of looking like a pathetic loser who couldn't stand up for himself was still much worse to me.

As if my self-image was not low enough, I also achieved the distinction of being considered the worst student in history. Not a joke, at all. Every student wanted teachers to curve their tests using my grade, often even before I had one. I was hoping that when I got to high school, the kids would have matured enough and the bullying would just go away on its own, but not a chance. Beating me was way too easy and evidently a lot of fun for many.

I knew what I had to do, but I was still afraid to do it. In preparation for ending the bullying, I honestly thought I was going to have to become something I never was, for the rest of my life. As it turned out, however, I had to become something I never was, for only about eight seconds. Then, after six years of torture, humiliation, and a lot of blood, I ended it all in approximately eight seconds. After those eight seconds, I was never touched again.

During the six years that I was bullied, I would ride my bike to Cross County Shopping Center in Yonkers and read every book I could in the self-help section of the book store. Reading these books made me forget the black-and-blues and broken nose, and they made me feel much better. And so, the knowledge with which I now communicate to all of you as "Love Story" was acquired as a result of my choices and reaction to being beaten almost daily for six years. The self-help books were the medicine that took away my pain, and it didn't take long for me to become addicted to them.

I guess I can say that, as a result of being bullied, inspirational books became my drug of choice.

My bullies and attackers have contributed immensely to giving me an incredible life. I'm truly grateful for everyone who put their hands in my face, for without them, there would be no Love Story, and I would probably have missed out on the daily joy I received from my most magnificent obsession. Even more than this are my many faithful readers whose lives might never have been touched if it wasn't for those who beat me. My writing did not become my life passion until more than thirty years after being bullied, so it was not easy for me to make the connection right away, but without being bullied, I don't know if I ever would have acquired the knowledge and passion for what I write about today.

I want to be clear that I am not advocating hurting yourself or anyone in any way, but even when I don't understand it, I know without any doubt that if something has "already happened," it happened to serve you, and there are no exceptions, including those situations we don't yet understand, and there are many I don't understand. I know that there are some really horrible things that happen in this world and I'm not asking you to like them. All I'm asking is that you trust. *Trust* that He has a plan for you and that whatever happens is for your realization, your becoming.

I wish I had the magic formula for you. I wish there were a way for every one of us to get to realization without experiencing some of the things we all go through, but I trust that what already has happened is the best thing for us.

As I sit here today and write these words, I'm in the most difficult position I've ever experienced in my entire life. At the very beginning, I was allowing it to destroy me, but that's all over now. And it's not because I don't care; it's because every day I give everything I have to completing what I was trusted to complete by finding ways to love the world, by working on myself, and by finding ways to make me more valuable.

I know why I lost all the money I was entrusted to protect. It happened because my soul knows that I (me, specifically) would not be able to endure living without making it right in my eyes. I would have had to either run, hide, lie, kill myself, or actually become someone I had been so successfully pretending to be for my entire life. The goal of every circumstance and situation is what we call *becoming more* and what our soul and God call *realization*.

Everything that happens, whether it is something you feel responsible for or something you feel was done *to* you, happens in your favor. The only reason that you can't see this is that you are concerned with what you missed out on, while your soul is only concerned with how what you missed out on will make you more.

THE ONLY CURRENCY THAT MATTERS

IT DOESN'T MATTER who you are or what you think you don't have, because whether you live in a castle or on the street, everyone has an unlimited supply of the only currency that matters. No budget is required for this currency. All you need to do is continue to find as many ways as possible to spend as much of it as you can, as many ways as possible to love your world. Love is the most valuable currency there is, and no one has more than you.

Love is when you get so much enjoyment from giving it away that you're neither aware, nor do you care, about what you receive.

I would like to end with one last story, or maybe I really wouldn't like to, but I've done such a good job of embarrassing myself so far, I figured, why stop? My greatest success ever might end up being how much I embarrass myself.

From the time I was a young kid to the present day, I have been and still am treated like gold by my parents. I would say that we were not wealthy, but we were more comfortable than average. I too could have lived a very comfortable life, but in retrospect and knowing what I know now, I'm glad I didn't. Instead, I pushed myself to insane limits in almost everything I did—and this is not an endorsement for something you should do. There are times for ridiculous persistence and times when you need to save yourself, a concept I have yet to grasp, evidently. I can't blame anything that has happened to me or that I did on anyone else. It was all me. When I say that I have failed more than anyone on this planet, I really believe that's true, but I was always rescued by my parents. I was literally "bought out" of almost all my failures. I honestly thought nothing could be more embarrassing than that, until recently. When this last and largest failure happened, when I lost all the money entrusted to me, initially I was devastated. I knew I would not go to anyone for help with this one. I thought it might actually kill my parents. I couldn't even talk to anyone about it, although I certainly would have accepted any help I might be offered, but who's going to offer if no one knows.

I went away. I chose to live in a place and in a way that I knew no one would understand, but somehow I knew that it was good for me. In this place, I discovered that I had never been saved; but instead, I had sold my identity over and over again. I wanted so badly to *be someone,* but I was quick to sell out the first chance I got by asking to be saved. I didn't know what I had been doing my entire life until I lived in a place with no people, no streets, no addresses, and no running water.

Finally, the silence told me the truth. My soul told me the truth—that my greatest failure was in fact my greatest blessing, but only if I was willing to accept the challenge I was receiving through *feeling.* I had to believe everything I write about at a whole new level. I had never thought of it that way. I only write what I believe, but now my journey was asking me to show *you,* and what could be more beautiful than that? I was scared to death when I started this book, but I knew what needed to be done.

It was not always easy to stay on purpose, especially in the beginning, but this process and dialogue have taken me to a very beautiful place. I tried to change my twenty-four-hour routine to reflect my level of belief and commitment and quickly learned that I wasn't able to go from what my day had been to what my day needed to be overnight. Instead, I had to progress in stages, but my dance with the universe had begun. Today, I have no questions and no doubts, although I know many others will, and I'm okay with that.

Eventually, when the shock of my failure had worn off a bit, I did tell some very close friends, and I was offered a possible solution. If it had been offered to me just three months earlier, I would have jumped at the chance. Instead, I politely and graciously declined, because I had come to understood how I was destroying myself. I sold who I was meant to become so I could be bailed out. My former serial solicitations for rescue missions had repeatedly damaged who I could have been in *our* terms and who I already was in my soul's terms.

I *know* that what I'm doing now is better, not only for everyone directly affected, but also for me. This is my chance to change the world and possibly have all my dreams come true in the process. I now thank God every day for what I used to call my "greatest failure," even though at the time I'm writing this it would still look to the world as if I have accomplished nothing.

This is not about me. Your greatest tragedy was meant to trigger something in you that would show you who you really are.

This is no longer a concept. This is now real. We know that what has already happened is the best thing that possibly could have happened simply because it *has* happened. And now, you no longer need to have blind faith. I am the proof. You don't have to just accept that whatever has happened is the best that could have happened simply because it has happened. Now, you have reasons to believe. The reasons are now clear, and I have the formula to help anyone convert their worst nightmare into their greatest blessing because that conversion is the reason it happened. It didn't happen because you're stupid or a failure. In fact, it happened to show you how brilliant you truly are. My intention is to communicate this in a way that you will understand me and grasp this truth. In reality, though, no conversion is going on, only enlightenment, only an understanding and awareness. Everything that has and still is happening to you is part of your journey, and all of it is beautiful, even those things you don't understand.

How can something so painful be beautiful? It is because *you* are so beautiful, and these moments reveal yourself to you.

I can try to explain it, and you can listen to me describe it, but only you can get yourself to experience what it's like to commit to something at such a high level that you can feel the universe moving in your favor. This is what it means to be connected. You feel like you're dancing with the universe.

You finally become aware that you have truly started living in the moment that you find something you're willing to die for.

This is My Soul executing God's plan for my realization. This is who I am, and this is what I get from asking the silence.

ABOUT THE AUTHOR

From His Friends

I've known Love Story since he was twelve years old and fell in love with him, then. He was my favorite student. I knew his family, as well, spending weekends with them, skating in Rockefeller Center and enjoying the city. I knew our connection was unusual and special, then, and it has survived the test of time. I did not see or talk to Love Story for twenty years, but suddenly we connected again and I met his beautiful family. We discussed metaphysical topics, which to my surprise were of interest to him. And here we are, now, with an insightful, instructive book from Love Story. Well, color me surprised but oh so delighted with Love Story's discoveries. I'm pleased to say that the student has become the teacher, which is as it should be in successful relationships. Do not miss this unusual and special man as he sincerely shares what he is learning from his unusual life.

—Dr. Lee Innocenti

ᜒ

Meeting Love Story after reading his words was interesting. He is animated, and his laugh makes anyone in earshot laugh, as well. He is intense and curious. As I listened to his stories about himself and loves lost, I thought, "What he doesn't know about women is a lot." Is it possible to be overly generous? He is. Is it possible to be too gullible? He is. It is sweet, but can lead to many unwarranted adventures. Love Story is both the character and the author. There are stories upon stories just waiting to be written and read.

The first time I read his page, I immediately knew that Love Story was a poet, the modern-day version of Oscar Wilde. "You don't love someone for their looks, or their clothes, or for their fancy car, but because they sing a song only you can hear." It sounds like Love Story, but it is Oscar Wilde from over two centuries ago. Oscar Wilde used his writings to express his pain. Love Story also writes therapeutically, expressing his observations and discoveries. Love Story also reminds me of Shakespeare. One famous quote from the bard reminds me of Love Story and his struggle to authenticity: "To thine own self be true, as the night the day, thou canst not then be false to any man." Love Story is on a mission to unravel truths that are a mystery to most of us.

Love Story's super-power would be love and his weapon or platform his writing. He is impossible not to like because he likes you. He is impossible not to trust because he trusts you. He believes every word you say to him and remembers it verbatim.

Some people will not agree with me, and I am biased. Yet, I did not know Love Story as a boy, as a young man, or as a married man. I know the Love Story of the present—father, writer, and trusted friend. I know Love story as the man he has evolved into and works daily to improve upon. I am thankful to be on the sidelines of his journey to enlightenment.

—Teresa DiRoberto, Teacher, Friend, Fan

I first met Love Story in a professional capacity, working as his freelance assistant. It struck me right away that he was different from any other client I'd worked for. My husband starting hearing about my "favorite client" almost daily, for Love Story always vocalized his appreciation for me and my value, and that is a big deal!

Love Story quickly became a trusted friend and mentor. He always sees the best in people and has an unwavering sense of optimism. He is impeccable with his word and always does more than he promises to do. If Love Story says something is going to happen, it happens—and even better than you may have expected. His words are more than backed by his actions. He is a big-hearted empath who constantly inspires and expands my vision for myself and challenges me in the best way. I look forward to seeing the amazing things he will do and accompanying him on that journey.

—Tiffany (and Jason)

∾

Chris Robinson on Love Story, his friend

I've had very few close friends over the years, but a lot of acquaintances, and the rarest and most beautiful thing is when an acquaintance becomes a friend and then a really dear friend. The ultimate is when a dear friend becomes your brother. That requires sharing deep feelings, respect, honor, honesty—and great humor. That "person" in my life is Love Story.

—"Brother Robinson"

Jacquie Robinson on Love Story

A magical thing happened one January day almost two years ago. Love Story landed in our lives—and turned them for the better. There aren't many people in the world I can say I always look forward to seeing, but Love Story is one. His smile is infectious. He

*is good-natured, decent, charming, and fun. He radiates kindness—
and, of course, love. I have no doubt that his quest to "unlock" love
will, in its time, make the world a better place. He's got a destiny,
and he wears it well. He's a master at "loving it forward," and he'll
always have a room in our house and in our hearts!*

✍

*Love Story came into our lives in an unconventional way. Looking
back now, years later, I realize that love and kindness are two words
synonymous with him. Little did we know that we were on the brink
of a wonderful friendship with a tremendously wonderful person.
Over the years, I have seen Love Story help many people. He is a
compassionate and gracious person who acts from love and expects
nothing in return. I have seen him make a big difference in people's
lives because he really cares for people. He realizes that a small act
of kindness on his part could make a world of difference for someone
who is suffering. Like a doctor, he takes away pain and suffering
and truly intends to make a positive impact on this world.*

*They say that angels walk among us and that we do not always
realize it. Love Story is one of those people. He has been nothing but
positive in his words and his actions. It seems the very essence of his
being is to bring people happiness. Geography and mileage do not
impede Love Story's ability to be present for all of our life moments. He
has been known to drive for hours just to meet a friend for coffee and
talk. Love Story goes beyond what most will do to bring kindness and
happiness to people. His smile is heartwarming. You can hear it in his
words. His positivity is contagious. This man we met by some wild
chance has worked his way into our hearts and has become family.*

—Eric and Maria

✍

How I met Love Story is a wild and crazy story in itself. I thank

God every day for dropping this amazing person in my path at exactly the right moment. It couldn't have happened more perfectly. I can't go into detail, but I'm beginning to think he's a being from another place. Love Story has been nothing but a constant encouragement to me, a bright uplifting to my day. Thank you, Love Story, my mentor, my friend.

—Jennifer Mitchell, Author, friend,
and mom of a Heaven Child.

∽

Love Story became part of my family over thirty years ago. I could always count on his contagious smile and positivity, no matter what was going on. Always ready with a helping hand, he never made others feel that they were imposing on him in any way. Not too long ago, I found myself in a very dark place and in need of someone to lean on. Love Story was there, without questioning, without judgment, and without any harsh words. He showed up with open arms and an open heart, ready to do whatever it took to help me find my way to the light. I am here today basking in the light of a beautiful, healthy life, in large part due to Love Story's faith in me and in the awesome power of love. I am a believer! Love Story, I pray that you continue your amazing work of bringing unconditional love into people's lives, one at a time, and that your "footprint" will forever change the world!

—Rita Droz

∽

I don't care what he did, I'll defend him!

—Gary Droz